QUANTRILL'S
RAID ON LAWRENCE, KANSAS

What Really Happened?

QUANTRILL'S
RAID ON LAWRENCE, KANSAS

Revisiting The Evidence

JAMES C. EDWARDS

SHOTWELL

COLUMBIA   So. CAR.

EST. 2015

PUBLISHING

Produced in the Republic of South Carolina by

SHOTWELL PUBLISHING LLC
Post Office Box 2592
Columbia, So. Carolina 29202

www.ShotwellPublishing.com

Cover Image: Col. William Clarke Quantrill (Cantey-Myers Collection)
Cover Design: Boo Jackson

ISBN: 978-1-947660-61-8

FIRST EDITION

10 9 8 7 6 5 4 3 2

Contents

PREFACE

It was 3 a.m., April 23, 1978, and I had just finished performing at a bar in Lima, Ohio. The last chord from "Play That Funky Music, White Boy" still rang in my ears as I packed up my guitar. For the past two years, I had played six nights a week, five hours per night, at clubs throughout the north central United States. But this night was different because it was my last performance. Tomorrow I was going home to Columbia, Missouri. While the bar gigs taught me a lot about the music business, I concluded the environment was not good for my mental or physical health, and I was ready to move on to something else.

Yet, I was clueless about what I was going to do. When I returned home, my mother handed me a book titled *Jesse James Was His Name* by William Settle. I hadn't cracked a book since college and figured I'd give it a shot. By golly, that book changed my life! Settle was the first to educate me about the fact that Civil War battles took place in Missouri. This was news to me because in elementary school, history texts said our state remained neutral and that all the fighting occurred in the eastern states. Boy, was I in for a surprise! Not only did I discover that Missouri had hundreds of battles and skirmishes, but that Frank and Jesse James were Confederate guerrillas involved in some of the fiercest fighting. Settle also introduced me to William Clarke Quantrill, the leader of the Missouri guerrillas. My interest in Quantrill led me to William E. Connelly's book *Quantrill and the Border Wars*, in which he excoriated Quantrill and his men.

Growing up in Columbia, it was hard for me to believe that good ole Missouri boys could be so brutal. I must have read Connelley's book a hundred times over a period of years — and believed every word of it. But after a while, I had an epiphany, and Connelley's version began to make no sense. For the first time, I started seeing numerous contradictions in his claims and accusations. This discovery inspired me to go back and research the primary sources regarding the guerrilla conflict between Missouri and Kansas. In doing so, I decided to focus first on the Lawrence Raid.

Rather than confirm Connelley's view about Quantrill's attack, I found many eyewitness accounts that were at odds with his story. Armed with this information, I concluded that my *raison d'etre* in life was to share my findings with the world. With the naivete' of a 4-year-old, I decided to write a book — however, it was soon apparent that I didn't know what the heck I was doing. It occurred to me that perhaps I could do a better job if I went back to school and studied history. Being a little 'long in the tooth,' I mustered up my courage and applied to graduate school at the University of Missouri-Columbia. Five years later, I earned my master's degree in history and a $10,000 student loan debt.

Filled with fresh confidence, I decided to take another shot at writing my book about the Lawrence Raid. This project and the resulting book have been a labor of love and taken many years, and miles driven, to complete. Yet, I'm excited about the information I've discovered.

Readers might assume from this study that I have a resentment toward Kansans, but nothing could be further from the truth. As a native Kansan myself, I have nothing but respect for the state, its history, and its people. I love the town of Lawrence and have paid hundreds of dollars in parking fines to prove it! During my research, I've had the good fortune of meeting and making friends with several locals. They have all been extremely kind and helpful.

The purpose of my book is to reveal the discrepancies in accounts that challenge the accuracy of the popular version of Quantrill's raid on Lawrence, Kansas.

INTRODUCTION

William E. Connelley wrote his defining biography about William Clarke Quantrill while he was president of the Kansas State Historical Society. Throughout his book *Quantrill and the Border Wars,* Connelley portrayed the guerrilla leader as a demented, psychopathic killer. Although Connelley posed as an unbiased historian, he revealed his goal of besmirching Quantrill's character when he wrote to a friend stating he was concerned that post-Civil War Missourians would make a hero rather than a scoundrel out of him. Connelley bragged that his book would derail their efforts and wrote, "I had in mind an object when writing this Quantrill book. I did not want the people of Missouri to make a hero of as bad a man as Quantrill was and think I have accomplished my purpose."[1]

So, why did Connelley set out to destroy Quantrill's character and reputation? The answer is likely found in his upbringing as a child. Born in Kentucky, Connelley's mother died when he was quite young, leaving his widower father to raise him. When the Civil War broke out, his father became a soldier in the Union army and fought for the duration of the war. This left Connelley an orphan until his father was mustered out of service. Unfortunately, when the elder Connelley returned home he was a broken man from his experiences during the conflict. These difficulties perhaps shaped his views about Southerners. Dr. Joseph Beilein says of Connelley, "Even as a child, he was likely aware of the irregular warfare that was rampant in the area (Kentucky) and may have felt that his family was besieged by antagonistic Southerners. Sometime in the 1880's he moved to Kansas, where the local populace reinforced his radical

---

1   Martin E. Ismert, *Quantrill-Charley Hart?* (Apache, OK: Young and Sons Enterprises, 1959), p. 14.

Unionist ideas. Connelley was a partisan who saw history as his battleground, a place to fight for just, moral, and right causes with little concern for accuracy or empathy. Books were the weapons used to wage this war."[2] When Connelley acquired information about Quantrill's life and career, he had all he needed to vent his hate and frustration on the South.

Many scholars were not fooled by Connelley's claim that he was unbiased. Dr. Albert Castel, author of *William Clarke Quantrill: His Life and Times,* commented, "This work [*Quantrill and the Border Wars]*, while extremely valuable for the information it contains, is seriously impaired by Connelley's extreme pro-Union, pro-Kansas and moralistic bias."[3] Historian Martin Ismert added, "There is no question but what the book was a clever piece of propaganda."[4] Despite these claims, subsequent Quantrill biographies fail to present any new information that disputes Connelley's paradigm.

Their views have never been questioned. Until now.

---

2   Joseph M. Beilein, Jr. *William Gregg's Civil War: The Battle to Shape the History of Guerrilla Warfare, (Athens, GA: The University of Georgia Press, 2019), p. 9.*

3   Albert Castel, *William Clarke Quantrill: His Life and Times,* (New York: Frederick Fell, 1962), p. 23n.

4   Ismert, p. 4.

Chapter 1

THE HISTORICAL ACCOUNT

POPULAR VERSION:

"All evidence shows that Quantrill was a cruel and unnatural child; that he was a degenerate; and that he was a criminal from childhood from choice. His sack of Lawrence, and murder there of near 200 helpless and inoffensive Kansas citizens, men, women and children, constitutes the blackest crime record in American history."

—William E. Connelley, Kansas Historian

Most contemporary historians believe that William Clarke Quantrill was an innate psychopathic killer, born on July 31, 1837, in Canal Dover, Ohio, to morally challenged parents. They say that in 1857, he moved to Kansas and taught school in Stanton. Quantrill then moved to Lawrence, Kansas, where he was accused to being a con man who played pro and anti-slavery groups against each other. When the Civil War erupted, Quantrill is said to have aligned himself with pro-Southern Missourians and formed his own independent guerrilla band. His command had no allegiance to either the Union or Confederacy. Quantrill's sole motivation was to engage in activities that personally benefited him.

As the story goes, on Friday, Aug. 21, 1863, Col. Quantrill led his Missouri guerrillas to Lawrence, Kansas. As the raiders entered the town, they came upon two Union camps. One belonged to the 2nd Kansas Colored, the other to the 14th Kansas Cavalry. The young and unarmed soldiers that locals referred to as infants and babes, were asleep when the guerrillas attacked, and the majority were gunned down.

The guerrillas then galloped down Massachusetts Street, killing indiscriminately. They surrounded the Eldridge House Hotel, whose occupants were unarmed civilians. Having no means of defending themselves, the guests quickly surrendered. The guerillas set fire to the Eldridge House and escorted the prisoners to a nearby hotel.

With the guerrillas in control of the town, Quantrill ordered his men to spread throughout town and kill everyone they encountered. Bloodthirsty, drunken raiders murdered men, women, and children. Many women were raped. Four hours later, Lawrence was engulfed in flames and approximately 200 unarmed, innocent men lay dead.

Later in the day, the Kansas cavalry drove the raiders out of their state and followed them into Missouri. In the following days, they tracked down and executed hundreds of guerrillas who participated in the raid.

This is the version of Quantrill's raid on Lawrence that history wants us to believe. However, there are witness accounts that conflict with this paradigm aand suggest that much information was altered, ignored, or hidden. This work focuses on presenting statements that conflict with the popular historical account of the Lawrence Raid.

Chapter 2

WHO WAS WILLIAM CLARKE QUANTRILL?

POPULAR VERSION:

"Quantrill was cruel and heartless."

— William Connelley, Kansas Historian

CONFLICTING VERSIONS:

"He seemed to be a very pleasant sort of fellow."

— Frank Smith, Missouri Guerrilla

"Quantrill was a modest, quiet, good-looking man with blue eyes, light hair, gentle of manner and courteous as well."

— Mrs. R. T. Bass, Missourian

William Clarke Quantrill conceived, planned, and executed the Lawrence raid. His rise from a nondescript soldier to the leader of the Missouri guerrilla movement is worth exploring.

COL. WILLIAM CLARKE QUANTRILL (CANTEY-MYERS COLLECTION)

BEGINNINGS (1857-1860)

Most sources agree that in 1857, Quantrill moved from Canal Dover, Ohio, to Stanton, Kansas, to teach school. In 1858, he became a teamster for Russell, Majors, and Waddell Freighting Company, based out of Leavenworth, Kansas. In this capacity, Quantrill accompanied Col. Albert Sidney Johnston's expedition to Salt Lake City, Utah, during his mission to put down the Mormon rebellion. While stationed at Camp Floyd, he heard that gold had been discovered at Pikes Peak Colorado and traveled there to try his luck at prospecting. Failing in this endeavor, Quantrill returned to Kansas and resided at the Whitney House in Lawrence. His residence at this hotel coincided with the period known as 'Bleeding Kansas', (1854-1860) when Free State and pro-Southern settlers were fighting each other to control the territories' political structure. Sources claim during this time that Quantrill was a con man who was playing the Kansans and Missourians against each other. They allege that he rode with Jayhawkers on their slave-stealing expeditions into Missouri, then alerting Missourians who, in turn, intercepted the Kansans at the state line.

But Quantrill's friend, W. L. Potter gave a different version of his occupation while in Kansas. Potter said that Quantrill worked as a spy for the pro-Southern Territorial Governor, Samuel Medary. Potter wrote, "We all understood Quantrill to say that he was in the employ of the Lieutenant Governor (technically, Territorial Secretary Hugh Walsh) as a detective, to find out the names of his Jayhawkers, & to capture [Charles] Jenison [sic]."[1] Jayhawker John Dean, who was duped into befriending Quantrill, confirmed Potter's story saying he was a "spie [sic] or detective in the interests of Slavery, and it may possibly be of the then Gov't...There could be no other conclusion than that Quantrill was acting the part of

---

1   William E. Connelley Collection: "Interviews and Correspondence Related to Quantrill and the Border War, *"Letters from W. L. Potter to W. W. Scott,* Box 13, Kansas State Historical Society, Topeka, KS. Herein referred to as Connelley Collection. (Samuel Medary was the Territorial Governor of Kansas from April 1857 to May 1858. He was a Democrat and was arrested in 1864 by Federal authorities for conspiring against the government. The office of Lieutenant Governor did not exist, but Medary's second-in-charge was his secretary, pro-Southerner Hugh Walsh.)

detective or spie [sic] in the pay or interest of the South."[2] Even though post-war Jayhawkers vehemently denied that Quantrill infiltrated their ranks, Dean claimed, "[Quantrill was] initiated into an order called 'Sons of Liberty' (forerunner of the Jayhawkers) in November 1860 at Osawatomie, by James Montgomery, the famous chief of southern Kansas."[3] Dean's statement is consistent with Missourian Andy Walker's recollection who wrote when Quantrill was warning him of an impending Jayhawker raid on his father's house, Quantrill said, "[He] had come from Osawatomie, Kansas, with three others, members of Montgomery's band, with the object of robbing my father of his slaves and stock."[4]

MORGAN WALKER RAID (1860)

Jayhawkers finally discovered that Quantrill was a spy and made plans to kill him. Quantrill heard about their intentions and organized one last excursion into Missouri. His purpose was to lead five Jayhawkers on a fallacious slave-liberating raid and have them killed (to disguise their Jayhawker membership, Connelley refers to them as Quakers, not Jayhawkers. They were both). On December 10, 1860, the incident took place at the home of Morgan Walker, a wealthy slave owner living near Blue Springs. Quantrill's ambush was successful, and three of the five Jayhawkers were killed.

QUANTRILL BECOMES A GUERRILLA (1861-1862)

After the raid, Quantrill realized he could no longer serve as a spy in Kansas and pledged his allegiance to pro-Southern Missourians. Marcus Gill, a wealthy slave owner living near New Santa Fe, Missouri, hired him to escort his slaves to Texas. On

---

2   William E. Connelley, *Quantrill and the Border Wars* (New York: Pageant Book Company, 1909), p. 134n.

3   Rev. John J. Lutz, "Quantrill and the Morgan Walker Affair," *Transactions of the Kansas State Historical Society,* Vol. 8, 1904, pp. 326n, 327n.

4   Joanne C. Eakin, Recollections of Quantrill's Guerrillas: As Told By A. J. Walker of Weatherford, Texas, to Victor E. Martin (Shawnee Mission, KS: Two Trails Genealogy Shop, 1996), p. 2.

Quantrill's return to Missouri, he stopped in the Indian Territory and lived with Cherokee chief Joel Mayes. When the Civil War erupted, Mayes' tribe organized a military company and aligned themselves with the Confederacy. The Cherokees elected Mayes as their captain, and Quantrill joined his command. The Indians attached themselves to Texas General Benjamin McCullough's Confederate army and were assigned to the Texas/South Kansas cavalry commanded by Colonel Elkanah Greer. Greer's company fought at Wilson's Creek and attacked the right flank of the Union army on Bloody Hill, where they were repulsed by cannon fire.

After the battle, Quantrill joined Missouri General Sterling Price's Confederate army (technically, Missouri State Guard) and fought at the Missouri battles of Dry Wood Creek and the siege of Lexington. When Price's army retreated, Quantrill stayed behind and joined a pro-Southern neighborhood protection militia based out of Independence, Missouri. In January 1862, Quantrill was elected captain and this group formed the nucleus of Quantrill's guerrillas. In the beginning, he commanded a total of eight men.

Quantrill Becomes A Confederate Captain

Early in the war, Quantrill's guerrillas fought alongside Missouri Confederate troops at the battles of Independence and Lone Jack, Missouri. However, their cooperation with Southern troops is disputed by many historians who believed the guerrillas were land pirates with no allegiance to the Union or Confederacy. Kansan W. K. Cone wrote, "[Quantrill's men] were not recognized by the Confederate army, nor were the guerrilla auxiliaries of the Southern cause."[5] Cone was unaware or ignored the fact that, on August 15, 1862, Col. Gideon Thompson mustered Quantrill and his men into the Confederate Army, Quantrill being commissioned Capt. of Scouts.[6] On April 28, 1862, the Confederate government further legitimized Quantrill's command by passing the Partisan Ranger Act. This document stated, "When as many as 10 men come

5   W. K. Cone, "The Quantrill Raid," in Adolph Roenigk (ed), *Pioneer History of Kansas,* 1933, p. 6. Kancoll.org/books/roenigk/chapt.2, htm.

6   Connelley, *Quantrill and the Border Wars,* p. 269.

together for this purpose, they may organize by electing a captain, 1 sergeant, 1 corporal, and will at once commence operations against the enemy without waiting for special instructions. Their duty will be to cut off Federal pickets, scouts, foraging parties, and trains and to kill pilots and other gunboats and transports, attacking them day and night, and using the greatest vigor in their movements."[7]

Quantrill's pro-southern friend, W. L. Potter, recounted Quantrill's mission as a partisan ranger officer: "His commission authorized him to go in Missouri, get all the recruits for the Army of the Confederacy, and give them all the assistance in his power on their way through the Federal lines, to our army...While inside of the Confederate Lines, him and his command were subject to the orders of the general commanding the district that he was in. When beyond the Confederate lines, he was at liberty to go where he pleased or in other words, was the commander of all the District that he could hold."[8] But Union authorities refused to recognize the Partisan Ranger Act and announced they would treat guerrillas (partisan rangers) as outlawed renegades. On March 13, 1862, Union Gen. Henry Halleck, commander of the Department of Missouri, issued Order No. 2 (aka: The Extermination Policy) which said, "They (guerrillas) will not, if captured, be treated as ordinary prisoners of war, but will be hung as robbers and murderers."[9] Interestingly, it should be noted that prior to this order, Quantrill paroled his Union prisoners, but afterward, he imposed his own 'no quarter' policy. After the battle of Lone Jack on Aug. 15, 1862, the victorious Southern army fell back to southwest Missouri, while Quantrill stayed behind. It wasn't long before he took the offensive and attacked the Kansas hamlets of Shawneetown, Paola, and Olathe.

At Olathe, Quantrill captured and paroled 125 Union Kansas troops, an unheard-of gesture between the two enemies, especially considering the guerrillas had just been outlawed. One of his

---

7   United States, *The War of Rebellion: A Compilation of the Official Records of the Union and Confederate Armies*. Series 1, Vol. 13, (Washington: Government Printing Office, 1880-1901), p. 835.

8   Connelley Collection, Letters from W. L. Potter to W. W. Scott.

9   Edward E. Leslie, The Devil Knows How to Ride: The True Story of William Clarke Quantrill and His Confederate Raiders (New York: Random House, 1996), p. 112.

LT. WILLIAM GREGG – MISSOURI guerrilla.
(FROM THREE YEARS WITH QUANTRILL BY BARTON)

prisoners, 2nd Lieutenant William Pellet, recalled Quantrill telling him, "I've been doing something the last half hour I very seldom do...I have come to the conclusion not to kill you...Now in a short time, my men are going to leave here...Before we leave, or about the time we leave, you get these men out of here."[10] After the war, William Gregg challenged the people of Lawrence: "I would like for some Lawrence man or woman to show me an instance where any Kansan ever acted with such magnanimity as did Quantrill in Olathe."[11] In the fall 1862, Quantrill led his command to Arkansas and united with Confederate Gen. Sterling Price's Missouri troops. Price assigned the guerrillas to Col. Joseph Shelby's Iron Brigade, who attached them to 1st Lt. Joseph Elliott's scouts of the 9th Missouri Cavalry. Quantrill then left his command for Richmond, Virginia, in hopes of receiving a Colonel's commission from President Jefferson Davis. The result of this meeting is unknown, as writers differ in their theories. We do know that when Quantrill returned from Virginia, Confederate officers referred to him as Colonel.[12] Before leaving, Quantrill appointed Lt. William Gregg to command his guerrillas. Gregg was a native of Jackson County, Missouri, and one of the first men to join Quantrill. Gregg's guerrillas fought alongside Price's Confederate troops at Cane Hill and Prairie Grove, (Arkansas), Springfield, Hartville, and Cape Girardeau, (Missouri).

In the spring of 1863, Quantrill returned to Arkansas and led his company back to Missouri. Upon his arrival, he began making plans to attack Lawrence. Quantrill knew the town was the home of many Kansas Jayhawkers and Red Legs. He believed Lawrence was a military threat to western Missouri that needed to be destroyed.

10 Ed Blair, *History of Johnson County, Kansas,* (Lawrence, KS: Standard Publishing Company, 1915), pp. 107, 196.

11 William H. Gregg, "A Little Dab of History without Embellishment," *Western Historical Manuscript Collection,* Columbia, MO, p. 28. (Hereafter called Gregg Manuscript).

12 Connelley, *Quantrill and the Border Wars,* p. 421.

MAKEUP OF THE MISSOURI GUERRILLAS

Historians continually demonize the men who rode with Quantrill, describing them as depraved individuals. One wrote, "Quantrill's men were essentially murderous thieves, utterly devoid of any social or political ideals who took advantage of the turmoil of the times to enrich themselves at the expense of their neighbors."[13] Civil War scholar Herman Hattaway added, "[The guerrillas were] the most notorious gang of psychopathic killers and plunder-mad marauders who ever roamed the prairies."[14] In contrast, historian Dr. Don R. Bowen conducted a demographic study of Quantrill's men and discovered that the vast majority were young men in their late teens and early 20s who belonged to the most wealthy, literate, and well-respected slave-holding families in western Missouri. Bowen maintained, "The guerrilla families constituted, in the main, an established rural elite."[15]

Once again, the reader sees the conflicting information regarding the guerrillas and Quantrill's life. So, which version have historians accepted as the truth? The reply comes by answering this question: who controlled the narrative after the war?

---

13 Don Bowen, "Guerrilla War in Western Missouri, 1862-1865: Historical Extensions of the Relative Deprivation Hypotheses." *Comparative Studies in Society and History,* Vol. 19, No. 1 (January 1977), p. 32

14 O. S. Barton, *Three Years With Quantrill: A True Story Told by His Scout John McCorkle,* (Norman, Okla.: University of Oklahoma Press, reprint, 1992), p. 10.

15 Bowen, p. 49.

Chapter 3

Kansas Invades Missouri

POPULAR VERSION:

> "There was not one of them [Red Legs] but performed valuable service for the Union cause, and, so far as I know and believe, always within the rules of civilized warfare... [They] did more to protect the homes of Kansas than any regiment in the service...."
>
> — Albert Greene, 9th Kansas Cavalry

CONFLICTING STATEMENTS:

> "[Red Legs were] sworn to shoot rebels, take no prisoners, free slaves, and respect no property rights of rebels or their sympathizers."
>
> — Henry Palmer, Captain, 9th Kansas Cavalry

> "[Red Legs will] shoot, kill, burn, and confiscate [in Missouri] until Lawrence [is] avenged."
>
> — Charles Jennison, Colonel, Jayhawker/Red Leg

Kansas Jayhawkers Invade Missouri

When the Civil War erupted, Kansas troops were absorbed into the Union Army. Many of these soldiers had previously fought as militia against pro-Southern Missourians during "Bleeding Kansas" and were eager to retaliate. One wrote, "The

13

tables are turned now; and here in camp are many Kansas men who were hunted in '55 and '56 by the Border Ruffians (pro-Southern Missourians). The Jayhawkers are now entering this State [Missouri] to settle up old scores...and bless the world with Christian civilization."[1] Gen. Jim Lane and Colonels Charles Jennison, James Montgomery, and Dan Anthony led the Jayhawkers. Their Kansas troops wasted no time attacking Missouri settlements along the western border.

By the end of 1861, the Missouri towns of West Point, Morristown, Osceola, Parkersville, Papinsville, Butler, Platte City, Dayton, Columbus, Kingsville, and Rose Hill had all been burned to the ground. Additionally, Independence and Harrisonville were sacked and plundered. One Jayhawker recalled, "In the neighborhood of Rose Hill, Jackson County, alone, forty-two houses were burned, and others robbed of their valuables."[2] Willard Mendenhall from Lexington, Missouri, witnessed Jayhawkers committing atrocities and wrote, "This is a reign of terror. Jennison's regiment is in the neighborhood. I am told they have burned two hundred private residences and shot several men...They have taken the lives of boys ten years old."[3] One Jayhawker remembered it was standard procedure for them to set fire to farmhouses, outbuildings, and crops. He added, "Any husbands or sons discovered would be tortured to determine the hiding places of valuables and then executed without ado. Whether the family was Unionist or Secessionist was a moot point: Missourians were Missourians, and all were vulnerable."[4] Political moderates back in Kansas were aghast when they heard about the Jayhawkers' behavior in Missouri. One lamented, "They are the offscourings of the New England states who were sent here

---

1   Thomas Goodrich, *Black Flag: Guerrilla Warfare on the Western Border, 1861-1865,* (Bloomington, IN: University of Indiana Press, 1995), p. 14.

2   S. M. Fox, "Early History of the Seventh Kansas Cavalry," *Collections: Kansas State Historical Society,* Vol. 11, 1909-1910, pp. 238-253.

3   Willard Hall Mendenhall, "Life is Uncertain: Willard Hall Mendenhall's Civil War Diary," *Missouri Historical Review,* Vol. LXXVIII, No. 4, July 1984, p. 444.

4   Don Gilmore, "Total War on the Missouri Border," *Journal of the West,* Vol. 35, No. 3, July 1996, pp. 70-80.

by the assistance of the emigrant aid society; and no worse class of wretches ever disgraced a country than they are generally. Had it not been for them we would have no difficulty here."[5]

Union officers also found the Jayhawkers' behavior despicable. Gen. H. W. Halleck, commander of the Department of Missouri said, "Jennison's men do not belong in this department. I have directed General Pope to drive them out, or, if they resist, to disarm them and hold them prisoners. They are no better than a band of robbers... They disgrace the name and uniform of American soldiers and are driving good Union men into ranks of the secession army."[6] Another person added, "There are miles and miles of Missouri thoroughfare, on the border, on which Jennison and his men burned every house and in many instances slaughtered the people."[7] One source added, "[Jayhawkers] have perpetrated unheard of crimes. Houses have been plundered and burned, defenseless men shot down and women outraged (raped)."[8] Writer Paul I. Wellman wrote, "The homes of friends and foes alike in Missouri which were plundered and destroyed by the Redlegs [sic] numbered in the thousands. No count has ever been made of the men and even women killed by the Kansas Outlaws."[9] A Kansas newspaper inquired, "Will Kansas never be rid of Jim Lane and Jennison?[10]

The Difference Between Jayhawkers And Red Legs

The reader should keep in mind that Kansas Jayhawkers and Red Legs are two separate organizations. The Jayhawkers were first organized during the 'Bleeding Kansas' era. This group was composed of radical northern abolitionists whose goal was to run pro-slavery

---

5   Allen T. Ward letter to Dear Sister, Oct. 27, 1861, Kansas State Historical Society, Topeka, KS, civilwaronthewesternborder.org/islandora/object/civilwar.

6   United States, Vol. VIII, p. 507.

7   Connelley, *Quantrill and the Border Wars*, p. 303n.

8   Leverett Wilson Spring, *The Prelude to the War for the Union* (Boston, Mass.: Houghton, Mifflin and Company, 1885) p. 287.

9 Paul I. Wellman, "Why Quantrill Sacked Lawrence," *Kansas Magazine,* 1939, p. 47.

10 Stephen Z. Starr, *Jenniison's Jayhawkers: A Civil War Cavalry Regiment and Its Commander* (Baton Rouge, LA: Louisiana State University Press, 1973), p. 249.

COL. CHARLES R. JENNISON – COMMANDER OF 7TH KANSAS CAVALRY (JENNISON'S JAYHAWKERS) AND 15TH KANSAS CAVALRY. FOUNDER OF RED LEG PARAMILITARYORGANIZATION. COURT-MARTIALED FOR CRIMES COMMITTED AGAINST MISSOURI. (WILSON'S CREEK NATIONAL BATTLEFIELD)

settlers out of Kansas. They later crossed into Missouri and began stealing slaves. Their leaders were John Brown, James Montgomery, John Stewart, Charles Jennison, and Jim Lane.

When the Civil War erupted, Jennison became Colonel of the 7th Kansas Cavalry. In 1861, his troops attacked several towns in western Missouri and burned them to the ground. They additionally murdered unarmed civilians, looted private property, and confiscated slaves. The 7th Kansas Cavalry adopted their pre-Civil War moniker, 'Jayhawkers,' and later became known as 'Jennison's Jayhawkers.'

Because of the atrocities Jennison's command committed in Missouri, the 7th Kansas Cavalry was transferred out of the Department of Missouri and sent east of the Mississippi River. Col. Jennison was court-martialed for his involvement in their crimes, and in May 1862, he resigned his commission.

Jennison then began recruiting for an independent cavalry organization that would be free from military control. His command was designed to be a guerrilla band that would be able to conduct missions they deemed important. Jennison's move was prompted by the fact that his Kansans wanted to fight Missourians and had no interest transferring east of the Mississippi River. Not surprisingly, most of Jennison's recruits came from the 7th Kansas Cavalry. With the prospect of being free from Union authority, many of the Seventh's members deserted or resigned to join Jennison's organization. Recognized by their red Morocco leggings, they assumed the moniker, 'Red Legs.' They were a secret organization that never submitted an official roster of its members.

Capt. George H. Hoyt was the leader of the Red Legs. Having served in the 7th Kansas Cavalry, he resigned to join Jennison. Hoyt established his headquarters at the Johnson House in Lawrence. Later, after Kansas political moderates outlawed the Red Legs, Captain S. S. Clarke, a survivor of Quantrill's raid on Lawrence, finagled a way to revive the infamous company. Clarke was a member of General Thomas Ewing's staff (Department of the Border), which gave him the authority to appoint Hoyt as the head detective for the army. In turn, Hoyt recruited his Red Legs as scouts.

The 15th Kansas Cavalry was organized in the summer of 1863, after the Lawrence raid for the purpose of retaliating against Missourians. Demonstrating they meant business, the bloodthirsty Jennison had his commission returned after he agreed to lead the command. Not surprisingly, many of his former Red Legs joined the organization. One source said that if the 7th Kansas Cavalry was known as Jennison's "Jayhawkers," then the 15th Kansas Cavalry should be remembered as Jennison's "Red Legs." The 15th Kansas was sent into western Missouri to enforce Order No. 11, a directive that depopulated the border area. Before entering the state, the Red Legs took an oath "to shoot rebels, take no prisoners, free slaves, and respect no property rights of rebels."[11]

---

11 H. E. Palmer, "The Black Flag Character of War on the Border," *Collections: Kansas State Historical Society, Vol. 9, 1906,* p. 464.

CAPT. GEORGE H. HOYT – 7TH KANSAS CAVALRY
(JENNISON'S JAYHAWKERS) AND RED LEG OFFICER. (WIKIMEDIA COMMONS)

THE CONFLICT BEGINS

Missouri was overrun with Union troops at the outbreak of the war, and the pro-Southern government retreated to Neosho, Missouri. In its place, a pro-Union provisional government was appointed by the United States government. This left pro-Southern families in western Missouri defenseless against Kansas Jayhawker and Red Leg attacks. These citizens desperately needed someone to step up and defend their rights and property.

William Clarke Quantrill would be that individual.[12]

---

12 For more information see Tom A. Rafiner, *Cinders and Silence: A Chronicle of Missouri's Burnt District, 1854-1870* (Harrisonville, MO: Burnt District Press, 2013).

CHAPTER 4

JAIL COLLAPSE: THE FINAL STRAW

POPULAR VERSION:

"[Kansas Lt. Cyrus Leland] is of the opinion that the girls were digging their way out of the jail."

— William Connelley, Kansas Historian

CONFLICTING STATEMENT:

"The death of these poor women crushed beneath the ruins of their prison was a deliberately planned murder."

— George Caleb Bingham, Missouri Artist

PRELUDE TO LAWRENCE ATTACK

On June 17, 1863, to address the guerrilla threat on the Missouri-Kansas border, Union authorities appointed Thomas Ewing Jr. to command the newly formed District of the Border in the Department of Missouri. Ewing, an Ohio abolitionist, moved to the Kansas Territory in 1858, and had an excellent reputation as an attorney. This resulted in him being appointed the first Chief Justice of Kansas. When the war broke out, Ewing received a Colonel's commission, and he commanded the 11th Kansas Infantry. Ewing and his men fought valiantly at the battles of Old Fort

BRIG. GEN. THOMAS EWING, JR. - COMMANDER, DISTRICT OF THE BORDER
(LIBRARY OF CONGRESS)

Wayne (Indian Territory), Cane Hill, and Prairie Grove (Arkansas). His new responsibility as commander was to protect Kansas from invasion and exterminate the guerrillas in western Missouri.

Ewing built military posts up and down the state line to protect the Kansas border. Each station was occupied by one cavalry company. The gaps between stations were roughly 10 to 12 miles apart, and cavalry squads were constantly on patrol. Ewing was confident that Kansas could not be invaded without first being detected by his border guards. This 'early warning system' would give him time to concentrate his cavalry and eradicate the invaders.[1]

Ewing took a three-pronged approach in dealing with the guerrillas. First, he created a counter-guerrilla organization and sent them into western Missouri. These troops would dismount in areas where high levels of guerrilla activity existed and wait in ambush.[2] Next, Ewing recruited spies to infiltrate the guerrilla ranks. Finally, Ewing took aggressive measures against the rural Missouri civilian population known to support guerrillas. Ewing said of these Southern sympathizers, "About two-thirds of the families...are of kin to the guerrillas, and are actively and heartily engaged in feeding, clothing, and sustaining them." To solve this problem, Ewing wrote, "I think that the families of several hundred of the worst of these men should be sent, with their clothes and bedding, to some rebel district south, and would recommend the establishment of a colony of them on the Saint Francis or White Rivers in Arkansas, to which a steamboat can carry them direct from Kansas City."[3]

Ewing believed this measure would prompt the guerrillas to follow their families to Arkansas. His idea became General Order No. 10. Missourians severely criticized Ewing's proclamation as it targeted male and female non-combatants. In hindsight, however, Ewing's decision to banish sympathizers is tactically correct.[4]

---

1   Posts were located at Atchison (KS), St. Joseph (MO), Iatan (MO), Weston (MO), Leavenworth (KS), Parkville (MO), Kansas City (MO), Westport (MO), Little Santa Fe (MO), Aubrey (KS), Coldwater Grove (KS), West Point (MO) Rockville (KS), Sugar Creek (KS) Trading Post (KS), Fort Lincoln (KS) and Fort Scott (KS).

2   Albert R. Greene, "What I Saw of the Quantrill Raid," *Collections: Kansas State Historical Society, Vol. 13,* pp, 27-28.

3   United States, Series 1, Vol. XXII, Part 2, p. 428.

4   Subsequent conflicts fought by the United States in Vietnam, Afghanistan, and Iraq prove that guerrilla warfare will continue to thrive unless the rural population is controlled.

JAIL COLLAPSE

Union troops began arresting civilians suspected of aiding guerrillas. One group of young women from Jackson County, Missouri, were family members of Quantrill's men. The exact number of women arrested is unknown, but it's believed between nine and eleven girls, all younger than 20, were in the group. One Missourian explained why they were imprisoned: "These families were arrested and confined under the pretext of holding them as hostage for the good behavior of their brothers, husbands or relatives, who were supposed to be in sympathy with, or actually engaged in the Confederate Cause."[5] The girls were held in a three-story building on Grand Avenue between 14th and 15th streets in Kansas City, where they occupied the second and third floors of the makeshift jail.

On August 13, 1863, the building collapsed, and six women were killed. The dead included Josephine Anderson (guerrilla Bill Anderson's sister), Susan Crawford Van Diver (cousin of Cole Younger; her husband Tom Van Diver and younger brother Riley Crawford both rode with Quantrill), Mrs. Armenia Crawford Selvey (a cousin of Cole Younger), Mrs. Christine McCorkle Kerr and Mrs. Nanny McCorkle (sister and sister-in-law of John McCorkle) and a Mrs. Wilson. Guerrilla Bill Anderson was deeply affected by the tragedy, as all three of his sisters — Josephine, Mollie, and Janie — were prisoners. After the dust settled, his oldest sister, 14-year-old Josephine, was found dead. Mollie's injuries crippled her for life, and 10-year-old Janie suffered two broken legs, a lacerated face, and an injured back. What caused the jail to collapse remains a mystery, but several theories have been presented. William Connelley said the women accidentally caused their death by attempting to tunnel out of the building. But his conclusion is problematic because the girls occupied the second and third floors — areas not close to the foundation.[6] Writer Charles Harris provides a more plausible story, saying the Kansas soldiers accidentally undermined the structure by tearing down a wall in the adjacent Cockrell building. Harris

---

5   *Washington Sentinel*, March 9, 1878.

6   Connelley, *Quantrill and the Border Wars*, pp. 300-301.

said the troops tore out interior walls for easier observation of the prisoners and, by doing so, put too much strain on one of the joists that ran through both buildings, causing the collapse.[7]

Another theory came from local Elijah McGee, who blamed Kansas soldiers for intentionally causing the disaster. Two days before the building collapsed, McGee entered the jail and saw evidence that the structure was being altered. In a sworn deposition, McGee testified that he "found that the Posts or Columns had been cut away from the girders or centre [sic] beam and that the Girders or Centre beam had already sunk down two or three feet and with his affiant feeling that the house was unsafe immediately left."[8] Quantrillians also accuse Kansas soldiers of purposely causing the collapse. They point out that the prison guards were members of the 9th Kansas Cavalry who had recently been ambushed by guerrillas near Westport. The company suffered many casualties and it's believed members sought revenge by undermining the building. One Missourian supported this theory, writing, "the death of these poor women crushed beneath the ruins of their prison was a deliberately planned murder."[9] The guerrillas' reaction was predictable. They believed the Kansans purposely murdered their loved ones and swore to avenge their deaths.

Guerrilla William Gregg said the jail collapse was the tipping point that prompted Quantrill to drop everything and attack Lawrence. Gregg wrote, "In my estimation, only for this cowardly act, the raid on Lawrence would never had occurred."[10] Guerrilla John McCorkle, whose sister and sister-in-law died in the collapse, agreed; "This foul murder was the direct cause of the famous raid on Lawrence, Kansas. We could stand it no more...We were determined to have revenge, and so, Colonel Quantrill and Captain Anderson planned a raid on Lawrence, Kansas, the home of the

---

7   Charles Harris, "Catalyst for Terror: The Collapse of the Women's Prison in Kansas City," *Missouri Historical Review,* Vol. LXXIX, No. 3, April 1995, p. 303.

8   State of Missouri, County of Jackson, Philip Brown, Notary Public, and Elijah McGee, Sept. 10, 1863.

9   *Washington Sentinel*, March 9, 1878.

10   Gregg Manuscript.

JOHN MCCORKLE AND T. B. HARRIS – GUERRILLA MEN.
BOTH LOST FAMILY MEMBERS IN KANSAS CITY JAIL COLLAPSE.
(FROM THREE YEARS WITH QUANTRILL BY BARTON)

leaders, Jim Lane and [Charles] Jennison."[11] Sadly, Connelley was unsympathetic to the guerrillas' plight, writing, "No, the guerrillas had no sufficient cause for the Lawrence Massacre."[12]

---

11   Barton, p. 123.

12   Connelley, *Quantrill and the Border Wars*, p. 297.

PLANNING THE ATTACK

Perhaps it was serendipity, but Quantrill was already busy making plans to attack Lawrence. As early as July 1863, William Gregg noted that Quantrill met with his officers at the Lilburn Goodloe farm near Blue Springs, Missouri, to discuss the possibility of attacking the town. This meeting lasted 24 hours as the officers hotly debated the feasibility of the raid. Quantrill informed his lieutenants he had recently received information from a 'prominent man' in Lawrence about the town's defenses. This unidentified person was most likely W. W. Lykins, a known pro-Southern sympathizer.

Quantrill told his officers he had personally reconnoitered into Kansas as far west as Eudora to inspect a bridge that crossed the Wakarusa River to determine if it could be used during a retreat.[13] He nixed the idea because the wooden bridge could easily be destroyed.[14] On August 10, three days before the jail collapse, Quantrill again met with his officers at the farm of Capt. James Perdee on the Blackwater River near Columbus, Johnson County, Missouri. He updated them about his nascent plan to raid Lawrence, but he still had no idea about when the attack might occur. When Quantrill heard about the death of the girls, he immediately sent runners to gather his command. On August 17 and 18, guerrillas companies belonging to George Todd, William Gregg, John Jarrette, John Brinker, Confederate Col. John Holt, Cole Younger, and Samuel Clifton began to arrive. On the night of August 18, the officers agreed to attack Lawrence. They planned to leave the following day, August 19.

GUERRILLA SPIES IN LAWRENCE

After the jail collapse, Quantrill met with one of his most valuable guerrillas. He was a black man named John Noland, a slave who was owned by Asbury Noland of Independence, Missouri. Some historians believe Asbury was not only his owner but his father.

---

13 *Ibid.*, p. 310.

14 *Kansas City Star*, July 19, 1903.

It's believed John had three white stepbrothers: George, Henry, and William, and when they joined Quantrill, he went along and worked as a hostler.[15]

Quantrill asked Noland to ride to Lawrence to inspect the town's defenses and troop strength. Noland recalled, "I being a colored man I had the advantage of any white man as a spy. Quantrill had sent a white woman to Lawrence before he sent me, but she failed...I counted one hundred and forty soldiers camped about the town, but a portion of those left the day I was there...I started for Lawrence about the 12th or 14th of August...I only spent one day and one night in Lawrence."[16] Kansas troops arrested Noland as he was returning to Quantrill and incarcerated him for ten days. He was therefore unable to pass his information on to Quantrill. When Noland failed to return, Quantrill sent Fletcher Taylor to Lawrence. Taylor roomed at the Eldridge House and represented himself as a cattle speculator. He left Lawrence on August 19 and reported back to Quantrill that night at the home of Benjamin Potter south of Lone Jack, Missouri.

Missourian A. J. Liddell also claimed that he went to Lawrence to spy for Quantrill. Liddell was a justice of the peace in Independence and had three sons riding with Quantrill. Liddell said he posed as a wounded Union soldier and boarded at the Eldridge House.

Testimony from raid survivors suggest there were other guerrillas in Lawrence spying for Quantrill. According to local Hovey Lowman, "He (Quantrill) had spies going and coming constantly to and from the city and knew much more accurately than most of its citizens just the preparation that was made for his reception. He was doubtless at all times in possession of as perfect a knowledge of the exact condition of the city — whether it was guarded or not, whether its citizens slept soundly nights."[17] Lowman wasn't the only

---

15 Donald R. Hale and Joanne Eakin, *Branded as Rebels* (Independence, Mo.: Wee Print, 1993), p. 326.

16 Connelley Collections, Statement of John Noland.

17 Hovey Lowman, *Narrative of the Lawrence Massacre on the morning of the 21st of August 1863*, Reprinted by the Watkins Community Museum of History, (Lawrence, Kan.: State Journal Steam Press Print, 1864), p. 32.

RICHARD CORDLEY – MINISTER, PLYMOUTH CONGREGATIONAL CHURCH. CORDLEY WROTE MANY ACCOUNTS ABOUT THE RAID. IRONICALLY, HE ADMITTED HE FLED WITH HIS FAMILY TO THE NORTH SIDE OF THE KANSAS RIVER. CONSEQUENTLY, HE DID NOT WITNESS ANY OF THE EVENTS HE WROTE ABOUT. (FROM HISTORY OF LAWRENCE, KANSAS BY CORDLEY)

one who saw suspicious people, as other locals recalled seeing spies the night before the raid. The Reverend Richard Cordley said that on the evening of August 20, the home of Hugh Fisher (chaplain for the 5th Kansas Cavalry and friend of Lane) was being watched. To substantiate his claim, Cordley wrote that when guerrillas went to Fisher's house, his wife told them he wasn't home. But one raider disagreed, saying he had watched the home all night and that no one had left the premises.[18] Other locals saw several strangers in

_____

18 *Kansas City Times*, Aug. 21, 1913.

town. One wrote, "Some ladies and gentlemen returning late the night before, saw horsemen stationed at the outskirts of town... The design was doubtless to notice if any messenger came in to warn of danger, and to be sure that no alarms was given."[19] Cordley also believed two guerrillas attended the railroad meeting held at the Eldridge House on August 20. He recalled during the raid, he overheard two guerrillas debating about whether Jim Lane was in town. When one guerrilla replied that he was out of town, the other said, "No he isn't, didn't I see him at the railroad meeting last night?"[20] Another local, Mrs. Sarah E. Lanton, claimed the night before the raid, she saw two men arrested for being suspected guerrilla spies. They denied the accusations and set free. Sarah saw these same men the next day during the raid.[21]

This information supports three important points. First, the Lawrence raid was not a knee-jerk response. It demonstrates that Quantrill was in the process of making plans to attack Lawrence, but the deaths of the women forced him to immediately retaliate. Second, there were people living in Lawrence who provided Quantrill with valuable information. Finally, the guerrilla chieftain knew more about the status of Lawrence than has been credited.

19　The Rev. Richard Cordley, "Quantrill's Raid on Lawrence, Kansas, Aug. 21, 1863." Reproduced for the 125th Anniversary of Quantrill's Raid on Lawrence, Kansas, p. 3.

20　*Ibid.*, p. 3.

21　*Lawrence Evening Tribune, May 10, 1886.*

CHAPTER 5

THE APPROACH

POPULAR VERSION:

"[John N.] Edwards says [Confederate Colonel John] Holt was with Quantrill at the inception of the raid but this is not probable."

— William Connelley, Kansas Historian

CONFLICTING STATEMENT:

"Colonel Holt was yet on hand with his forty men [at the Blackwater camp]."

— Andy Walker, Guerrilla

SIZE OF GUERRILLA COMMAND

For years historians have debated the number of guerrillas who participated in the Lawrence raid; estimates range from 175 to 600. William Gregg, the guerrilla quartermaster, reported that 294 men participated in the attack.[1] Guerrilla Andy Walker added that Confederate Colonel John Holt and his 40 recruits were included in that number.[2] Testimony from numerous raid survivors agrees with Gregg's account, saying that no more than 300 men attacked the town. Local Rev. Cordley confirmed, "The number of men with Quantrill has been variously estimated. Some have placed it as

---

1 Gregg Manuscript.

2 Eakin, p. 57.

high as six hundred and some as low as one hundred and seventy-five. There is no reason to question the substantial accuracy of the statement – that two hundred and ninety-four answered roll call at Lone Jack before starting. All the testimonies concur in making the number of the raiders about three hundred."[3]

Cordley's statement should have settled the issue, but Connelley came up with another figure. He claimed that 50 Missourians from the Grand River area joined the guerrillas near the state line and that Confederate Col. Holt added 104 recruits near Chapel Hill, Missouri. Connelley insisted that 448 men participated in the raid.[4] This is another example of Connelley creating his own conclusions and ignoring witness testimony.

WAS THERE CONFEDERATE COLLUSION IN PLANNING THE RAID?

The timing of Holt's Confederate troops joining the guerrillas is a delicate issue because it either implicates or absolves the Confederacy of colluding with Quantrill's plan to attack Lawrence. For his part, Connelley wanted readers to believe Quantrill acted independently and without Confederate authority. He maintained that Holt's men accidentally ran into Quantrill's command 'en route' to Lawrence and was unaware of their murderous intent. However, Andy Walker maintained that Holt was at Quantrill's Blackwater camp with his 40 troops.[5] If Walker is correct, Holt's presence is evidence that perhaps the regular Confederate army was complicit in the raid. This begs the question; was Holt ordered to participate with Quantrill and if so, how far up the Confederate ranks did the collusion go? Most historians absolve former Missouri governor Confederate General Sterling Price of complicity because they believe that he was too noble and honorable to be involved

---

3   Richard Cordley, *A History of Lawrence, Kansas: From the Earliest Settlement to the Close of the Rebellion*, (Lawrence, KS: E. F. Caldwell, *Lawrence Journal Press*, 1895), p. 237.

4   Connelley, *Quantrill and the Border Wars*, p. 315.

5   Eakin, p. 57.

BRIG. GENERAL AND SENATOR JAMES H. LANE –
HID IN CORNFIELD DURING RAID. (LIBRARY OF CONGRESS)

in such a brutal affair. Raid survivor Fred Read added, "I do not assert that the Confederate authorities were in any way responsible for the Quantrill massacre. Be it said to the honor of the Southern Confederacy that no authorized Confederate soldiers participated in the slaughter. Some Confederate soldiers were indeed among the guerrillas, but the evidence goes to show that they were here from personal choice and not by official orders."[6]

There is, however, a fly in the ointment. After the raid, General Price defended the guerrillas' attack on Lawrence and had his adjutant write Quantrill, "General Price is very anxious that you prepare the report of your summer campaign...He wants to have all the facts clearly portrayed, so that the confederacy and the world may learn the murderous and uncivilized warfare which they (Jayhawkers) themselves inaugurated, and thus be able

---

6   "Memorable Meeting" newspaper clipping, 1891, and List of Quantrill's Raid Survivors, Lawrence, Kansas. www.kansasmemory.org/item/225627/page/24.

to appreciate their cowardly shrieks and howls when with just retaliation the same measure is meted out to them."[7] Price's remark worried Connelley, who wrote, "It is to be hoped that it will never be established that General Price approved the Lawrence Massacre, but his letters must speak for themselves."[8]

Additionally, a few individuals made remarks that suggest Confederate complicity. For example, on his deathbed, Quantrill said, "My instructions (implies orders being given) were to first search that house and find Jim Lane if possible."[9] Lawrence survivors also recall Quantrill telling them he had been ordered to destroy Lawrence in retaliation for Osceola. Guerrilla Cole Younger wrote that General Joseph O. Shelby ordered the raid and that Quantrill carried it out.[10] Last, on their way to Lawrence, a guerrilla told a guide, "This is Marmaduke's command and Quantrill is in the lead."[11] (Connelley wrongly rewrote this quote to say the guerrilla said, "This is 'Quantrill's' command").[12]

AUGUST 19, 1863

On the morning of August 19, the guerrillas rode west. Andy Walker said the men had no idea where they were going and recalled, "When the order was given to break camp and saddle up...not many knew where we were going, but all felt that serious business was at hand."[13] With 16 guerrillas dressed in Union uniforms, George Todd led the advance while Quantrill rode in the column's rear. Quantrill sent scouts out to protect his flanks, and they reported back to him on an hourly basis. The command's pace was intentionally slow as several Union camps were in the area. Contradicting Connelley's

---

7   United States, Series 1, Vol. 53, p. 908.

8   Connelley, *Quantrill and the Border* Wars, p. 437n.

9   *Morning Herald,* Lexington, Ky., March 21, 1898.

10   *Kansas City Post*, March 21, 1915.

11   Cindy Higgins, "Kidnap of Jacob Rote," *Where the Wakarusa Meets the Kaw: A History of Eudora, KS, 2015,* www.Eudorakshistory.com/civil_war.

12   Connelley, *Quantrill and the Border Wars*, p. 328.

13   Eakin, p. 57.

claim that no Kansas troops were in Missouri, the following information documents the Union commands and their locations in western Missouri:

Lexington, Missouri

    1st Missouri State Militia Cavalry

Warrensburg, Missouri

    1st Missouri State Militia Cavalry

Pleasant Hill, Missouri

    11th Kansas Cavalry

    4th Missouri State Militia Cavalry

Independence, Missouri

    11th Kansas Cavalry

    4th Missouri State Militia Cavalry

Harrisonville, Missouri

    6th Kansas Cavalry

    1st Missouri State Militia Cavalry

    4th Missouri State Militia Cavalry

Westport, Missouri

    5th Kansas Cavalry

    6th Kansas Cavalry

    9th Kansas Cavalry

Little Santa Fe, Missouri

    9th Kansas Cavalry

    4th Missouri State Militia Cavalry

It was 5 p.m. when the guerrillas arrived at the home of Benjamin Potter located just south of Lone Jack, Missouri. The command had traveled only a paltry 10 miles. Quantrill did not want his command to be discovered by Union soldiers, so he took his time negotiating his way towards Kansas. Under normal conditions, horse riders would have covered this distance in 1½ hours instead of six, as horses trot at an average rate of 6½ miles per hour.

While at the Potter home, the guerrillas fed their horses and ate a light dinner. Fletch Taylor rejoined the command, having just returned from Lawrence, and reported that an attack was favorable. With this information, Quantrill assembled his men and told them they were going to Lawrence. He said, "You, one and all, will understand that the undertaking we are about to commence is one of extreme hazard. It might be that the entire command will be overwhelmed, the ranks decimated as they have never been before. Hence, I say to one and all, if any refuse to go they will not be censured."[14] Gregg said that no one deserted the ranks while Castel believed 12 guerrillas rode off[15]. Guerrilla Frank Smith recalled two men leaving.[16] At 8 p.m., the raiders mounted and headed toward Kansas.

AUGUST 20, 1863

The guerrillas rode non-stop for the next 11 hours, and on August 20 at 7 a.m., they arrived at the headwaters of the Middle Fork of the Grand River, just south of present-day Belton, Cass County, Missouri. They rested here for the next 10 hours near the farm of Nathan R. Harrelson. At 5 p.m., the guerrillas remounted and headed towards Kansas, 4 miles away. At 5:30 p.m., the guerrillas crossed the state line.

Capt. Joshua A. Pike of the 9th Kansas Cavalry (a resident of Lawrence and former disciple of extremist John Brown) commanded 100 troops at Aubrey, Kansas. His company consisted of soldiers from the 9th and 11th Kansas Cavalry. In his official

---

14 Gregg Manuscript.

15 Castel, p. 124.

16 Frank Smith Manuscript, notes taken by Albert Castel in possession of the author.

CAPT. JOSHUA A. PIKE – 9TH KANSAS CAVALRY
(FROM "PIKE'S STATEMENT" CONNELLEY)

report, Pike wrote that at 5:30 p.m., he received information that an unknown cavalry force was crossing into Kansas. Pike wrote, "[Quantrill] passed about five miles south of our camp. He gave it out that he was going to Paola to join United States troops there. He was representing that he was a Union officer, commanding Union troops himself."[17] Pike discovered his mistake about an hour later and sent warnings north to Little Santa Fe, Westport, and Kansas City, Missouri. He also alerted the military post at Coldwater Grove, Kansas, roughly 12 miles to the south. Sadly, Pike failed to send warnings to the interior towns in Kansas.

---

17 J. A. Pike, "Quantrill's Raid on Lawrence, Kansas: Statement of Capt. J. A. Pike Concerning the Quantrill Raid," *Western Historical Manuscript Collection,* University of Missouri-Columbia.

CAPT. CHARLES COLEMAN – 9TH KANSAS CAVALRY
(FROM BLOODY DAWN BY GOODRICH)

In his official report, Pike said he could not hinder Quantrill's movement as he only had 21 soldiers at his post. He instead sent a messenger to Capt. Charles F. Coleman at Little Santa Fe, Missouri, instructing his company to reinforce him. Coleman's command included 100 men in the 9th Kansas Cavalry. Coleman promptly complied with Pike's request, but it was 10 p.m., 4½ hours later, before he reached Aubrey. When he arrived, Coleman reported that Pike had 100 soldiers, not 21, mounted and ready to ride. It was midnight when the consolidated commands began their pursuit of the guerrillas.

William Gregg's recollection of entering Kansas differs from Pike's. Gregg maintained the guerrillas crossed a half-mile, not 5 miles, from Pike's post. This location makes sense, as a road from

Missouri into Kansas exists at this point, whereas there was not one 5 miles south. Gregg also said that Pike mounted his entire garrison and rode out on the prairie to confront the guerrillas. Gregg wrote, "[W]e again resumed our march to Lawrence crossing the state line in half mile of Aubrey, where two hundred federal troops were quartered. In the bright sunlight of the evening, these troops rode out on the prairie, formed and watched us march by."[18] After the war, a reporter confronted Gregg and pointed out that Pike's report didn't agree with his statement. Gregg responded, "He [Pike] said he never saw us but he did. He could have prevented the Lawrence raid right there."[19] Yet, in an interesting twist, guerrilla Frank Smith said he didn't see Union troops when they crossed the state line.

Rev. Cordley blamed Pike for causing the Lawrence debacle and wrote, "[Quantrill] crossed over into Kansas about five o'clock in the afternoon. They passed in plain sight of a camp of United States troops some miles away at Aubrey. The troops did not attempt to intercept them. It would have been madness to do so, as the raiders outnumbered them four or five to one. This camp was in command of Captain J. A. Pike. He sent word at once to Kansas City, but why he did not also send word to Lawrence has never been explained."[20] Connelley also criticized Pike saying, "If he had reported that he saw Quantrill in Kansas, marching west within a mile and a half of his garrison, and that he did nothing, he would have been court-martialed, as he should have been."[21] The most damning report came from the *Council Grove Press,* who wrote that when Quantrill's command entered Kansas, two of Pike's men asked permission to notify Lawrence but were denied.[22] While the truth will never be known, Captain Pike suffered severe consequences for his decision not to send warnings to Lawrence and harass Quantrill's flanks. General

---

18 Gregg Manuscript.

19 *Kansas City Post*, Aug. 23, 1914.

20 Cordley, A *History of Lawrence, Kansas: From the Earliest Settlement to the Close of the Rebellion*, p. 192.

21 Connelley, *Quantrill and the Border Wars*, p. 315n.

22 *Council Grove Press*, Sept. 14, 1863.

Thomas Ewing wrote, "Unhappily, however, instead of setting out at once in pursuit, he (Pike) remained at the station, and merely sent information of Quantrill's movement to my headquarters, and to Captain Coleman, commanding two companies at Little Santa Fe, 12 miles north of the line. Captain [C. F.] Coleman, with near 100 men, marched at once to Aubrey, and the available force of the two stations, numbering about 200 men, set out at midnight in pursuit. But Quantrill's path was over the open prairie, and difficult to follow at night, so that our forces gained but little on him. By Captain Pike's error of judgment in failing to follow promptly and closely, the surest means of arresting the terrible blow was thrown away, for Quantrill would never have gone as far as Lawrence, or attacked it, with 100 men close on his rear."[23]

After the guerrillas crossed the state line, two of Ewing's spies, riding with the guerrillas, deserted and rode towards Kansas City to warn headquarters of the attack. Unfortunately, Kansas troops spotted the men and mistaking them for guerrillas, fired at them. Fearing they would be shot before being able to identify themselves, the spies were forced to take a longer route to Kansas City, where they didn't arrive until midnight.[24]

There are two issues in this chapter that can be debated. The first is whether the Confederacy sanctioned the raid on Lawrence or if Quantrill acted independently. Second, was Captain Pike a coward by permitting Quantrill to pass without confrontation or were the guerrilla's miles away out of his view?

---

23   United States, Series 1, Vol. 22, pp. 579-585.

24   G. W. E. Griffith, *My 96 Years in the West: Indiana, Kansas and California* (Los Angeles: G. W. E. Griffith, 1929), p. 129.

CHAPTER 6

THE ROAD TO LAWRENCE

POPULAR VERSION:

"Perhaps the most heroic effort to save the doomed city was made by a Shawnee Indian, Pelathe."

— William Connelley, Kansas Historian

CONFLICTING STATEMENT:

"Afterwards, it transpired that this messenger got lost [and] rode several miles out of his way...The man fled back to Kansas City, and never boasted of the service rendered on that night's lonely ride on the timbered Kaw bottom to Lawrence."

— H. E. Palmer, 9th Kansas Cavalry

GUERRILLA STOPS ALONG THE ROAD TO LAWRENCE

It was 7 p.m. on the night of August 20, when Quantrill halted his men a few miles south of Squiresville, Kansas, a well-known Red Leg outpost. He sent a death squad to the home of Col. Charles Sims, a Union refugee from Missouri. This sortie would be the first of many, as several pro-Union Missouri refugees moved to Kansas for safety. Sims was fortunate not to be home.

As the command rested, Quantrill gave supplemental orders to his men and said, "I want you to burn every house in Lawrence and kill every man; but if a man in this command insults a woman and I find out, I'll hang him to the first tree I can get him to."[1] Another guerrilla recalled Quantrill saying "that they would be ordered to burn every house in town. He [Quantrill] had some friends in the town that had conferred favors on him in former days, that they and their families and their property also should not be molested. That his men could not and must not kill boys under 16 years of age. That it was their privilege to take any kind of property, including watches and jewelry, from the women. But they must not under any circumstance shoot any women or children. That if any of his men insulted a woman in that town, or violated her honor, that he would hang him to the first tree he could find."[2]

The guerrillas reached Spring Hill at 9 p.m. and Gardner at 11 p.m. Kansas soldiers occupied both towns, but as the guerrillas were wearing Union uniforms, the troops made no effort to halt them. Stephen J. Wilson, a Gardner resident, remembered the guerrillas riding through town: "It was in the evening when Quantrill's men passed through the town on their way to sack and burn Lawrence. They moved quietly along, riding four abreast, with pickets out in all directions, the officers speaking to their men in a clear deep undertone, saying 'Close up, close up'...They claimed to be new troops going to Leavenworth to be mustered into service."[3] West of Gardner, the command stopped at the home of Missouri fugitive, Dr. W. W. Shean. His wife told the guerrillas her husband wasn't home, but she had seen them approaching and told the doctor to go outside and hide in the brush. Consequently, Shean's son, Edwin, was forced to guide the guerrillas to the road that led to the Bluejacket Crossing. Edwin complied, and having completed his task, returned home.

---

1   Eakin, p. 59.

2   Connelley Collection, Letters from W. L. Potter to W. W. Scott.

3   Blair, p. 144.

Wilson recalled his friend's escapade. "Edwin P. Shean, then a boy, was induced to put the Johnnies (guerrillas) on the right road to Lawrence and was their guide for a few minutes. He was not harmed, is alive yet, and lives on a farm near Gardner. No persons were tortured, no shots were fired, no one was killed and no houses were burned in Gardner."[4]

DEATH OF GUIDES?

Sources claim Quantrill was unfamiliar with the territory outside Gardner and kidnapped a total of 10 guides to help him navigate through the area around Captain's Creek. Gregg recalled, "A guide was procured. He had not been with us over thirty minutes, however, until someone recognized him as a former resident of Missouri and shot him down. In the next eight miles there were at least ten who met the fate of the first guide procured."[5] However, some historians believe Gregg's claim is nonsense, because every victim associated with Quantrill's approach to Lawrence is identified except these ten men. Guerrilla Frank Smith added to the controversy saying he knew of no guides being killed on their way to Lawrence.[6]

THE HOMES OF BENTLEY, JENNINGS, AND STONE

Before crossing Captain's Creek, the guerrillas came upon the home of Private William Bentley, a member of the 12th Kansas Infantry. They surrounded his house and ordered the inhabitants outside. Bentley was not home, but two of his comrades were staying there overnight. The soldiers believed the guerrillas were their friends, and as they came out, the raiders fired on them. One soldier was killed while the other was wounded and escaped into the timber.[7] The guerrillas then stopped at the home of Augustus Bromelsick, a Missouri German refugee. Bromelsick and his hired

---

4   *Ibid.*, p. 144.

5   Gregg Manuscript.

6   Frank Smith Manuscript.

7   Connelley, *Quantrill and the Border Wars*, p. 326.

hand, Mr. Klingenberg, were suspicious of the men at their door and hid in the cellar. The guerrillas discovered their hiding place and led them upstairs. Bromelsick blew out a candle and escaped in the dark while Klingenberg broke free from his captors and ran into the brush.

AUGUST 21, 1863

It was 3 a.m. on August 21 when the guerrillas crossed Captain's Creek and passed through the German town of Hesper. They halted at a crossroads called Keystone Corner, just south of Eudora, where two men on their death list lived. One was Capt. Andrew Jackson Jennings, an officer with the 12th Kansas Infantry. His commanding officer was Col. Charles W. Adams, son-in-law of the hated Jayhawker, Gen. James H. Lane.

Col. Adams and his 12th Kansas Infantry had a bad reputation. In 1862, 300 of Adams' Jayhawkers invaded western Missouri and stole property and slaves. On their return to Kansas, Missouri Union troops attacked and forced them to surrender at gunpoint. The Missourians made the Jayhawkers return the stolen property and the officers, including Adams, were temporarily incarcerated and reprimanded.

When the guerrillas knocked on Jennings' door, his wife, Rose, explained that her husband was away at Fort Scott, Kansas. However, a neighbor disputed her claim, saying that Col. Jennings "was away in a hold, in their cellar."[8] After a search of the house came up empty, another squad rode over to the home of Joseph Stone. Stone was a Missouri refugee who had years earlier been responsible for the arrest of George Todd. Although texts portray Stone as a civilian, another source maintained, "Both Mr. Stone and his son were in the Union Army, and no doubt were on Quantrill's list to be killed en route to Lawrence."[9] Frank Smith recalled the

---

8   Glen Freeman, *Freeman Collection of Hesper, Kansas History Records,* Lawrence, KS, Kenneth Spencer Research Library Archival Collections.

9   Adela Hunt Davis, "True Stories about Pioneer Days, as Told to Her Grandchildren," *Freeman Collection of Hesper, Kansas History Records.* Lawrence, KS, University of Kansas, Kenneth Spencer Research Library Archival Collections, 1970, pp. 17-19.

older Stone was wearing his Union uniform when captured. Stone's son saw the guerrillas approaching and escaped out the back door. When the guerrillas captured the elder Stone, they yelled, "We've got you, old man, this time, sure ... get your clothes; you've got to go with us."[10] Stone was taken to Todd, who wanted to shoot him on the spot, but Quantrill wouldn't permit weapons to be discharged this close to Lawrence. Todd told his men to fetch a rope so he could hang him, but they failed to find one. One guerrilla found an empty musket inside Stone's house and brought it to Todd. While sources say Todd took the butt of the weapon and clubbed Stone to death, others believed guerrilla Sam Clifton, whose loyalty to the South was questioned, was ordered to take the musket and kill Stone.[11] Before leaving Keystone Corner, the guerrillas detained 16-year-old Jacob Rote and took him to Quantrill. Rote had been staying with the Stone family, and Quantrill inquired if he knew the way to Lawrence. Responding in the affirmative, Rote was remounted on a fine horse and put at the head of the command.

On their way to Lawrence, a guerrilla asked Rote, "Young man, do you know who you are riding with?" Rote responded, "No, and I don't care, so long as you treat me well." The guerrilla replied, "This is Marmaduke's command, and Quantrill is in the lead."[12] Rote led the guerrillas to Lawrence and held horses during the raid. Before leaving town, Quantrill dressed Rote in new clothes and sent him home. Afterward, Rote joined Jennison's 15th Kansas Cavalry and fought for the duration of the war. He was later murdered in Eudora by the brother of a comrade.[13]

---

10   *Kansas City Star*, Aug. 19, 1903.

11   Joseph K. Houts, *Quantrill's Thieves* (Kansas City, Mo.: Truman Publishing Co., 2002), p.64.

12   Cindy Higgins, *Eudora's History*, www.Eudorakshistory.com. (May 23, 2019).

13   *Kansas City Star*, Aug. 19, 1903.

FAILED WARNINGS

After the guerrillas left the Jennings home, Rose ran to the house of William Guest and begged him to ride to Lawrence to warn the inhabitants of Quantrill's presence. Guest didn't believe her story and went back to bed. However, Guest's black servant, Henry Thompson, volunteered to walk to Eudora to alert authorities. As he trekked towards town, he halted Frederic Pilla, a justice of the peace, who was returning to Eudora from a wedding ceremony. Upon hearing about the guerrillas, Pilla drove to town, roused the citizens, and asked for volunteers to warn Lawrence. Three men responded to his plea; they were David Kraus, Casper Marfelius, and Jerry Reel. The men quickly mounted and set off in the dark towards Lawrence. Unfortunately, Kraus' horse stumbled and fell, severely injuring him. The other two men continued until Reel's horse also stumbled and crushed him to death. His companion, Marfelius, stopped to tend to Reel. Consequently, Lawrence failed to receive a warning of the raid.[14]

One Kansan disagreed with the timing of the night riders' event. Responding years later to a request from Connelley for information leading up to the Lawrence raid, Oscar G. Richards wrote, "They (Marfelius, Kraus, and Reel) did not start until Lawrence had been sacked and the Bushwhackers had gone South."[15] One other attempt was made to alert Lawrence. When Ewing's spies informed Colonel Preston Plumb about Quantrill, Pelathe', a Delaware Indian, volunteered to ride and warn the town. Theodore Bartles, a known Red Leg, escorted him to Six Mile House (a Red Leg headquarters) and gave him his horse. Pelathe failed in his attempt to warn Lawrence, but the reason for his failure is debatable.

The popular story states Pelathe rode this horse at breakneck speed until it faltered; then sacrificed it by cutting a gash into its flank and pouring gunpowder into the wound. This prompted the horse to bolt in pain for a few more miles until it pitched dead from

---

14 Connelley, *Quantrill and the Border Wars*, pp. 330-331.

15 *Ibid.*, p. 331n.

MAJ. PRESTON B. PLUMB – ADJUTANT, GENERAL THOMAS EWING'S STAFF.
(WILSON'S CREEK NATIONAL BATTLEFIELD)

exhaustion. Pelathe was then said to run on foot, where he arrived at the north side of the Kansas River opposite Lawrence just as the guerrillas entered.

There is, however, a less complimentary version of Pelathe's story. It says: "[Plumb] had sent a messenger to Lawrence. Afterward, it transpired that this messenger got lost, rode several miles out of his way, and finally reached a point near Lawrence in time to see the charging hosts of Quantrill's band filling the streets of the doomed city. The man fled back to Kansas City, and never boasted of the service rendered on that night's lonely ride on the timbered Kaw bottom to Lawrence."[16]

---

16   Gen. William Henry Sears, "The Paul Reveres of the Lawrence Massacre," *Kansas Collections,* Vol. 17, 1901, pp. 838-841.

THE FINAL DISTANCE TO LAWRENCE

After Quantrill crossed the Wakarusa River at the Blue Jacket crossing, he became familiar with the surroundings. It was 4 a.m. when the guerrillas reached Franklin, just 2 miles south of Lawrence. There was a small garrison of Union troops stationed here, but the soldiers ignored the guerrillas. As they passed, a witness heard one officer shout, "Hurry up; we ought to have been in Lawrence an hour ago. Rush on, boys; it will be daylight before we are there."[17] Dr. R. L. Williams, a Franklin resident, said the guerrillas halted briefly and that he walked amongst them without being harmed. Williams noticed many were strapped to their saddles to prevent them from falling from their horses while they slept. Gregg remembered arriving at Franklin: "The crowing of the cock warned us of the near approach of daylight, and it being our desire to reach Lawrence not later than sunrise, the horses were hurried to a long trot. Franklin was reached just at dawn — barely light enough to distinguish a soldier from a citizen, several of whom we saw cross the street in front of us. The command was here thrown into a column of fours and put to a gallop."[18]

At 5 a.m., the guerrillas reached a summit to the southeast overlooking Lawrence.

---

17 Connelley, *Quantrill and the Border Wars*, p. 328.

18 Gregg Manuscript.

CHAPTER 7

THE FORTIFICATION OF LAWRENCE

POPULAR VERSION:

"Lawrence was unprotected and helpless."

— William Connelley, Kansan Historian

CONFLICTING STATEMENT:

"Lawrence had from two to three hundred Militia, well-drilled and well-armed with plenty of ammunition."

— Cosma Colman, Private, 14th Kansas Cavalry

LAWRENCE FORTIFICATIONS PRESENT ON AUGUST 21, 1863

Most survivor accounts adamantly claim that the people of Lawrence were helpless and defenseless. S. S. Clarke wrote, "[The attack]...was a conspiracy to murder the people of a defenseless city, far removed from the lines of contending armies."[1] Another survivor, Fred Read, added, "[Quantrill] was the leader of a conspiracy to destroy a defenseless city and murder a defenseless

---

1   "Memorable Meeting" newspaper clipping, List of Quantrill Raid Survivors, (May 23, 2019), p. 24.

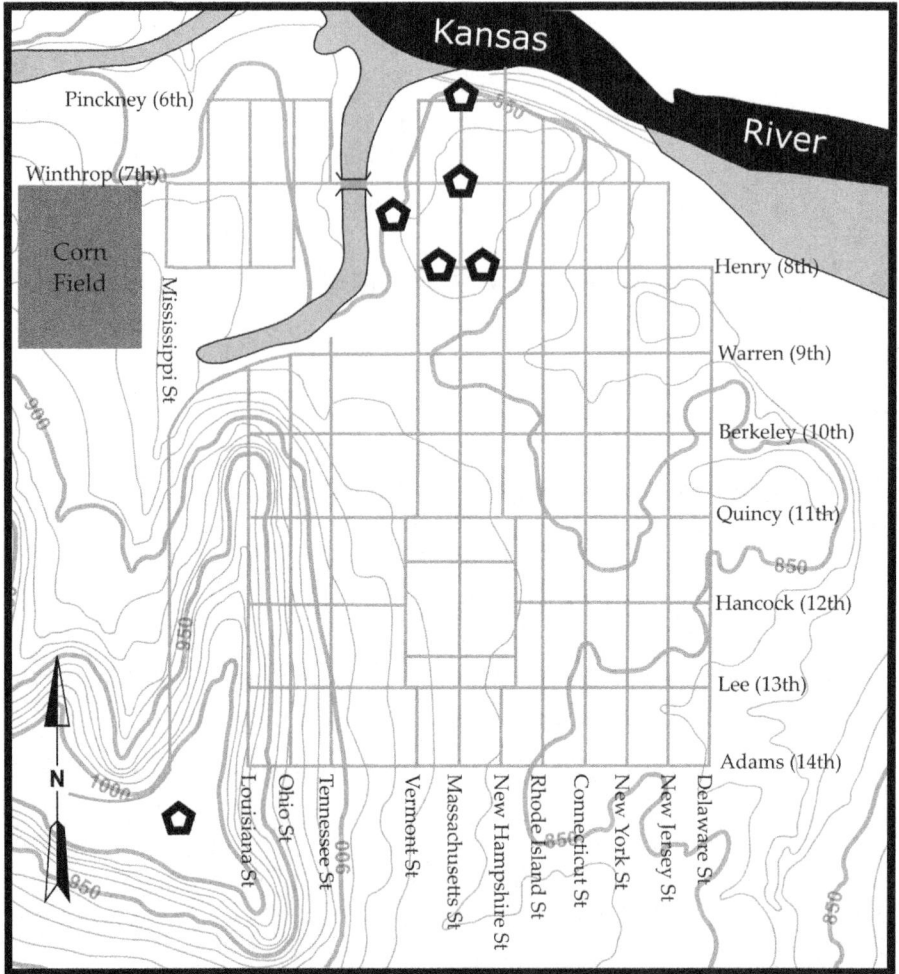

MAP OF LAWRENCE FORTIFICATIONS – AUGUST 21, 1863, AS DESCRIBED BY PRIVATE COSMA COLMAN, 14TH KANSAS CAVALRY. (CIVILWARMUSE)

people."[2] In contrast, however, Dr. Steve Jansen, former curator for the Douglas County, Kansas Historical Society, wrote, "Lawrence, a community of over 2,000 people, had a well-drilled independent militia, an armory with 50-60 guns and two reinforced blockhouses at two different intersections in the heart of the town. Why weren't they able to mount a better defense?[3] The truth is, on August 21, 1863, Lawrence, more than any other town in Kansas, was prepared to meet and defeat an attack on their town.

AVAILABLE WEAPONS

RIFLES AT THE LAWRENCE ARMORY

It's known that at least 60 rifles were inside the armory located across from the Eldridge House. However, the historical record maintains the weapons were 'old and rusty' and not battle-worthy. But simple logic suggests this can't be true. The proof comes from an incident that occurred one week before the raid. At this time, Union authorities warned Lawrence of a possible guerrilla attack. This information prompted Gen. Collamore to mobilize his militia and have them man their fortifications.

When the guerrillas failed to appear, the militia was told to stand down. Yet locals bragged that if the guerrillas had come, they would have been annihilated.[4] Interestingly, they make no mention of old and rusty rifles. In fact, Richard Cordley wrote, "Had Quantrill's gang come according to promise, they would have been welcomed with bloody hands to hospitable graves."[5] So, if the muskets were in good order a week before the raid, why wouldn't they be functional a few days later?

---

2   *Ibid.*

3   Steve Jansen, "How Could It Have Happened?" *Douglas County Historical Society Newsletter* (Lawrence, KS, Watkins Community Museum of History, July-August 2001), p. 1.

4   Richard Cordley, "The Lawrence Massacre," *The Congregational Record* (Lawrence, Kan.: Vol. 5, Nos. 9 and 10, September and October 1863), pp. 98-115.

5   *Ibid.*

Skeptics also question whether the armory was the only location where weapons were stored. Information suggests there were other dispensaries in town. They include D. W. Palmer's store, the Eldridge House Hotel, and at privately-owned residences.

RIFLES AT D. W. PALMER'S GUNSMITH SHOP

Major Leroy J. Beam, the recruiting officer for the 14th Kansas Cavalry, said his troops had access to rifles near their bivouac. His camp was located between Massachusetts and New Hampshire streets, just north of 9th Street. The guerrillas attacked this position at 5 a.m. while the soldiers slept. Eighteen of the twenty-two soldiers were killed in the assault.

Major Beam wrote that his rifles were located just twenty yards away from camp. He said, "The muskets ... were stacked in the building not three rods (20 yards) from my company."[6] According to city maps, the building located three rods away was owned by a gunsmith, D. W. Palmer. Again, survivors claim these rifles were in disrepair, but Beam makes no mention of it in his report. To the contrary, he actually predicted "...had these men (14th Kansas Cavalry) had these arms they could and would have formed a nucleus to which the citizens would have rallied and the record might have been different."[7]

WEAPONS AT THE ELDRIDGE HOUSE HOTEL

The Eldridge House Hotel is also thought to have been another location where weapons were stored. After the guerrillas surrounded the hotel, Capt. Alexander Banks, provost marshal of Kansas, hung a white sheet from a second-floor window and surrendered the building. He told Quantrill, "We are defenseless and at your mercy."[8]

---

6   Richard B. Sheridan, "Editor's Comment," in Richard B. Sheridan (ed.) *William Clarke Quantrill and the Lawrence Massacre: A Reader,* (Richard B. Sheridan, Lawrence, KS, 1995), p. 328.

7   *Ibid.,* p. 328.

8   Connelley, *Quantrill and the Border Wars*, p. 343n.

Banks' claim about not having weapons is confirmed by a guest who recalled, "On an informal consultation it was found that there were only two muskets that had been retained, contrary to orders, by members of a military company, but without ammunition. What revolvers were in possession of the guests were found to be in much the same condition as the muskets."[9] However, there is testimony that contradicts this claim. Resident Sara Robinson recalled many rifles being stacked in a room on the first floor of the Eldridge House.[10] She wrote in her memoir that Gen. Collamore required "every man (serving as militia guards) to leave his gun stacked in the N. W. room in the Eldridge House when he went home."[11] Another source reported that "plenty of arms were available [in the Eldridge House], but the timid guests surrendered."[12] And, proving that soldiers in the hotel were armed, one guest recalled an officer, on hearing the hotel had surrendered, "found his brace of revolvers, like his uniform, only a dangerous encumbrance."[13]

Capt. Banks fails to mention in a letter to his brother that the lack of weapons was the determining factor for him surrendering the hotel. He wrote, "I had thrown on my uniform, with the first intention of rallying some of the men and giving them a fight, but a little reflection convinced me that even if we could make a stand in the house they would fire the drugstore beneath and roast us alive or shoot us as we ran out."[14] Survivor H. B. Leonard also maintained that weapons were stored at the Eldridge House. He said Robert L. Frazier, owner of a drug store located at the north entrance of the

---

9   R. G. Elliott, "The Quantrill Raid As Seen from the Eldridge House" as described by R. G. Elliott, Vol. 2, *Publications: Kansas State Historical Society Embracing Recollections of Early Days in Kansas, 1920,* pp. 185-186.

10   Sheridan, Sarah Robinson, "The Governor's Wife Recalls the Raid," p. 205.

11   *Ibid., p. 205.*

12   Unidentified newspaper clipping, Aug. 23, 1963, (Lawrence, KS: Douglas County Historical Society).

13   Elliott, p. 186.

14   Letter from Alexander Banks to Brother, Lawrence, KS, Douglas County Historical Society, Sept. 9, 1863.

hotel, secretly hid a cache of pistols inside his business. Leonard added that a week before the raid, one of Quantrill's spies purchased revolvers from Frazier's store.[15]

A 12-Pound Cannon

Hovey Lowman is the only survivor to admit that Lawrence had a 12-pound cannon located on Massachusetts Street just north of the Eldridge House. He wrote, "On the opposite corner, north, was situated the Court House, a large building constructed of wood. The cannon watched by the side of this latter building."[16] Lowman added that as he watched the guerrillas charge down Massachusetts Street, he lamented, "But alas, no vigilant gunner with ready fuse watched by the side of the cannon."[17] Lowman also said two or three more cannon were inside Fort Lane on Mount Oread, but his claim cannot be confirmed.

Weapons Owned By Local Men

Many Lawrence men thought it was foolish for Collamore to store all the rifles at the armory. Concerned for their own safety, they secretly purchased arms and kept them at home. A review of testimony reveals that no fewer than 31 locals admitted to having weapons but chose not to use them. One was S. A. Simpson, who carried his Sharps rifle and 30 cartridges of ammunition into a corn patch where he hid from the guerrillas. Survivor Hiram Towne admitted he had a weapon, writing, "I dressed myself and took my shotgun, powder, and buckshot and went downstairs."[18] Survivor Col. John K. Rankin was armed along with his cousin, Capt. William Rankin, and witnessed other locals with weapons. He recalled seeing a group of men, thought to be guerrillas, riding down Vermont Street. Rankin recalled, "Just then three

---

15 Connelley Collection, Statement of J. B. Leonard.

16 Lowman, p. 48.

17 *Ibid.*

18 *Daily Journal-World,* Lawrence, Kan. Aug. 17, 1940.

or four [Lawrence] men who were there on Massachusetts Street fired several shots toward the supposed guerrillas."[19] Rankin also noticed a heavily armed militiaman heading downtown to confront the guerrillas. Sara Robinson added that Gen. George Dietzler was armed and wrote, "General Dietzler was trying to get his revolver just right to pick one of them off."[20]

DEFENSIVE FORTIFICATIONS IN LAWRENCE

THE ELDRIDGE HOUSE AS A FORTIFICATION

Nothing suggests that the Eldridge House was built as a defensive fortification, as was its predecessor, the Free State Hotel burned by Missourians in 1856. But testimony suggests soldiers would have manned it in the event of an attack. Historian Everett Spring wrote, "[the Eldridge House] could have been successfully defended by a dozen armed and resolute men against the attacks of horsemen whose heaviest ordinance was revolvers."[21] Survivor Hovey Lowman elaborated, "a few resolute men would have held the passage up into the Hotel against as many assailants as could have crowded into it. The passage led up a flight of stairs ten or twelve feet wide from the ground to the second story. The first doors were solid, and it would have required heavy implements to batter them down. Before that could have been accomplished, with the facilities at the command of the guerrillas, the head of the stairs could have been so obstructed that it would have been impossible for them to have reached the landing without first exposing themselves to the aim of the defenders."[22]

---

19   Connelley Collection, Statement of John K. Rankin.

20   Sheridan, Robinson, "The Governor's Wife Recalls the Raid," p. 208.

21   Spring, p. 291.

22   Lowman, p. 50.

Entrenchments And Blockhouses

Pvt. Cosma Colman and survivor Hovey Lowman are the only survivors who admitted that Lawrence had defensive fortifications. Colman affirmed, "Four entrenchments were thrown up; one across Massachusetts Street, near its confluence with Pickney (6th), two of circular form near Henry Street (8th), designed as a protection to those who have charge of Sharpe's [sic] rifles (thus admitting that Lawrence had Sharps rifles) and so arranged as to command Mount Oread, where it is presumed the enemy would plant their artillery and one on Vermont Street."[23] Colman added, "There were two blockhouses, one of them on the corner of Mass and Winthrop Streets (7th)."[24] Kansas Col. John K. Rankin confirmed the existence of a blockhouse near the Eldridge House, writing that during the raid, "I passed across the lot toward Vermont Street towards the blockhouse which then stood just north of where the hotel now stands."[25]

Lowman prepared a map that pointed out the location of the forts. He said that a "John Brown" fort was in the middle of Massachusetts and Henry (8th) streets and a "Judge Wakefield" fort positioned just west of Louisiana and Hancock Street (12th). He also recalled that earthworks were thrown up to the north of Henry Street (8th) and Kentucky Street. Lowman added that three forts were located on top of Mount Oread.[26]

Fort Lane On Mount Oread

Survivor testimony also fails to acknowledge a fortification located on top of Mount Oread. One source described the fort; "Mount Oread in 1863 was a scene of an ominous-looking network of trenches and breastworks, preparations for an anticipated

---

23 William G. Cutler. *History of Kansas*. www.Kancoll.org/books/cutler, Pt. 8.

24 Sheridan, Cosma Torrienta Colman, "The Massacre of the Union Cavalry Recruits," p. 198.

25 Connelley Collection, Statement of John K. Rankin.

26 Lowman, (map in appendix).

Fort Lane on Mt. Oread. (from Free State Fortress *by* Crafton*)*

Confederate attack."[27] On the day of the attack, guerrilla William Gregg confirmed, "Mount Oread was then the site of a Free State Fort."[28] At the time of the raid, no Kansas troops were stationed inside the fort.

MILITARY PERSONNEL

UNION TROOPS AVAILABLE

While survivor testimony maintains Lawrence was without defenders, research identifies no fewer than 52 Kansas soldiers in town on August 21. The troops consisted of 22 recruits of the 14th Kansas Cavalry and 20 soldiers with the 2nd Colored Kansas Infantry. Ten soldiers from the 12th Kansas Infantry were stationed on the north side of the Kansas River next to the ferry (Pvt. Colman

27 University Daily Kansan, April 17, 1961.

28 Gregg Manuscript.

EARTHERN FORTIFICATION IN LAWRENCE – LAWRENCE ILLUSTRATION
DRAWN IN IN 1856 BUT REPRESENTS WHAT FORTIFICATIONS LOOKED LIKE IN 1863.
(FROM FREE STATE FORTRESS BY CRAFTON)

believed they belonged to the 10th Kansas infantry). In an effort to hide the presence of soldiers in Lawrence, Sara Robinson referred to them as a 'survey team.' Edward P. Farren added that these soldiers were being trained as sharpshooters. He said, "For two or three weeks previous to the raid they had been recruiting a company of sharpshooters in Lawrence and they were camped in North Lawrence by the old Baldwin Mill."[29]

Testimony also indicates a company of Union cavalry was thought to be in the vicinity on the day of the raid. [30] Witnesses recalled that when they first saw the guerrillas south of town, they mistook them for Kansas cavalry. One said, "They thought [the guerrillas] were Union troops, as...a company of one of the Kansas

---

29 *Lawrence--Today and Yesterday,* Magazine and Souvenir Edition, Commemorating the Semi-Centennial Memorial of the Lawrence Massacre, published by the *Lawrence Daily Journal- World,* p. 123.

30 Sheridan, Robinson, "The Governor's Wife Recalls the Raid," p. 206.

regiments was expected in that city."[31] Local William Brown saw the troops and was told by a friend they belonged to the 2nd Kansas Cavalry.[32] Sara Robinson thought they were a company of the 9th Kansas Cavalry and said, "Captain [George] Earl and many of his [9th Kansas Cavalry] officers made their homes in Lawrence and their arrival would have certainly sealed the fate of the guerrillas."[33]

KANSAS OFFICERS HIDING IN THE ELDRIDGE HOUSE HOTEL

Most accounts fail to mention that an unknown number of Union officers occupied the Eldridge House when it surrendered. One guest recalled, "Although we had with us some officers in the military service, none had the ill-fortune to be in uniform."[34] Another source said the Eldridge House was full of "officers and soldiers on furlough."[35] Rather than fight to the death, they surrendered to Quantrill, enjoyed his protection, and survived the raid. Officers known to be at the hotel included Capt. Alexander Banks, Maj. Edwin Bancroft, Capt. F. W. Swift, Ansom Storm (Free State Militiaman), Maj. John Wilder (Free State Militiaman), Lt. Andrew Shannon, Capt. William Hazeltine, Col. John Rankin, Maj. J. B. Abbot, Capt. Frank Swift, and Gen. Carmi Babcock. If there were others, their names have been lost or forgotten.

UNION OFFICERS PRESENT DURING LAWRENCE RAID

No fewer than 38 Union officers were present in Lawrence on the day of the raid but failed to defend the town. They include but are not limited to, Gen. George Deitzler, Col. John K. Rankin,

---

31 Lowman, p. 45.

32 Connelley Collections, Statement of William Brown.

33 Sheridan, Robinson, "The Governor's Wife Recalls the Raid," p. 206.

34 Sheridan, J. M. Winchell. "The Sacking of Lawrence," p. 174.

35 Cone., Roenigk (ed), p. 9.

GEN. GEORGE W. DEITZLER –
1ST KANSAS VOLUNTEER INFANTRY
(WILSON'S CREEK NATIONAL BATTLEFIELD)

MAJ. SYDNEY S. CLARKE –
WRONGLY DESCRIBED AS CIVILIAN.
(NATIONAL ARCHIVES)

Capt. George Hoyt (a Red Leg), Gen. Carmi Babcock, Ma. Edwin Bancroft, Lt. Col. W. A. Rankin, Capt. S. F. Clarke, Col. Frank Swift, Capt. A. Shannon, Capt. Alexander Banks, and Lt. T. J. Hadley.

LOCAL MILITIA

To augment the Union force in Lawrence, Mayor and Gen. George Collamore organized a local militia comprised of battle-tested men. Many had experience fighting pro-Southerners during the 'Bleeding Kansas' period. His militia also included former Union soldiers. One local said of the force, "[Collamore] organized an effective military company and secured arms for them from the state. He also organized and armed companies in the country about Lawrence."[36] Another wrote, "The men of Lawrence organized into military companies and drilled daily, and the women worked at

---

36 Cordley, *A History of Lawrence, Kansas,* p. 183.

home or met to make cartridges for the soldiers... Lawrence had 550 soldiers drilled and ready."[37] The *Lawrence Journal* stated that Lawrence had more than 500 men prepared to defend the town.[38] Pvt. Cosma Colman recalled, "All that summer, Lawrence had from two to three hundred Militia; well-drilled and well-armed with plenty of ammunition."[39]

THE LAWRENCE SCARE AND TOWN PREPAREDNESS

As previously mentioned, a week before Quantrill's raid, Lawrence was warned that an attack was imminent. Collamore mobilized his local militia and called in its members from surrounding counties. A company of the 11th Kansas Cavalry, from Fort Riley, under the command of Maj. Edmund G. Ross, was deployed to Lawrence. With these troops, the *Lawrence Journal* boasted, "No enemy can come within ten miles of Lawrence before we know it."[40] Resident Hovey Lowman agreed, "The citizens were armed and converted into soldiers. Two or three militia companies were ordered from the county, and they, joined with the armed citizens, made a formidable force. ...The cannon, full-shotted, watched for the enemy down Massachusetts Street."[41]

The townsfolk were confident their forces would defeat an attack. One newspaper bragged, "Mr. Quantrill is not invited to do bloody and infamous deeds upon unarmed men in any part of this state, but we venture to say that his chance of escaping punishment...are indeed slim — perhaps more so than in another town of the state."[42] Another wrote, "Lawrence is safe. The beleaguered City of Martyrs, at last...is in such condition of defense that we only fear that the cowardly guerrilla will not penetrate

---

37 Cutler, Part 8.

38 Sheridan, *Editor's Introduction, Lawrence Journal* p. 135.

39 Sheridan, Colman, "Massacre of the Union Cavalry Recruits," p. 198.

40 Sheridan, *Editor's Introduction, Lawrence Journal,* p. 135.

41 Lowman, p. 32.

42 *Lawrence Kansas State Journal,* Lawrence, KS, Aug. 6, 1863.

GEN. GEORGE W. COLLAMORE – MILITIA COMMANDER AND LAWRENCE MAYOR. (WILSON'S CREEK NATIONAL BATTLEFIELD)

even to the suburbs."[43] Lowman believed the town was ready and said, "At the appointed time [when Quantrill was anticipated to attack], Lawrence was in a condition to have defended itself against twice the number that he could have brought against it."[44] Hiram Towne added, "If we could have had one hour's notice we could have saved the city...[the guerrillas] were planning to come a week before but we got word of it and were prepared for them. They found out and didn't come." When the guerrillas failed to attack, Hadley's troops were ordered to Fort Leavenworth, and the militia was told to stand down.

Given the resources of men, weapons, and fortifications, many Union authorities were disappointed when Lawrence failed to defeat Quantrill's forces. Union General Ewing wrote, "[Lawrence] had an abundance of arms in their city arsenal, and could have met Quantrill, on half an hour's notice, with 500 men."[45] Another wrote, "They had the arms and the men to have defended the place and drive the murderers back, if not to have destroyed them."[46] Another witness concurred that "there were plenty of weapons in Lawrence and brave men to use them."[47] Pvt. Cosma Colman added, "[Lawrence] succeeded in having a company of troops raised in this town, the militia was drilled, blockhouses had been built, and everything was in readiness...It would have been impossible, if Quantrill had had twice that number of men, to have gotten into the city."[48]

Colman predicted if the town had been given 20 minutes' notice, "many of them (guerrillas) would never have returned and but few citizens killed." He supported his opinion saying that "twelve men in the Block House could have commanded the then entire

---

43 *Leavenworth Conservative,* Leavenworth, KS, Aug. 4, 1863.

44 Lowman, p. 32.

45 United States, Series 1, Pt. 1, p. 583.

46 *The Independent,* Oskaloosa, Kan., Aug. 29, 1863.

47 Cone, Roenigk (ed), p. 7.

48 "Stories of the Survivors: From Addresses Made on Wednesday Evening at the Reunion in the Bowerstock Theatre," Lawrence, KS, University of Kansas, Kenneth Spencer Research Library.

business portion of the town and could have killed and repulsed them (guerrillas) as fast as they came."[49] Local Sarah Fitch added that "a half hours' notice would have saved all."[50] Another survivor wrote, "An hours' warning would have been sufficient and we could have driven them all away, if we could have had only an hour's warning — we had not a moment."[51]

As can be seen, survivors of Quantrill's raid did not want anyone to know of the troops, weapons, and fortifications available on the day of the attack. All, except for two survivors, conveniently failed to address the topic and continued to maintain they were defenseless and helpless. While this made for good propaganda in the North, it was certainly not the truth. Sadly, this was only the beginning of the inaccuracies written about the raid.

---

49 Sheridan, Colman, "The Massacre of the Union Cavalry Recruits," p. 198.

50 *Postmarked: Bleeding Kansas: Letters from the Birthplace of the Civil War, Pioneer dispatches from Edward and Sarah Fitch*, (Lawrence, KS: Purple Duck Press, 2013) p. 269.

51 Letter from John Stillman Brown to John L. Rupur, Sept. 1, 1863. *Kansas Memory*, Kansas State Historical Society. www.kshs.org/km/facets/view/facets:890, 4060,1184 .

CHAPTER 8

ATTACK ON KANSAS SOLDIERS

POPULAR VERSION:

"[The guerrillas] murdered 20 of the Second Kansas Colored Volunteers."

– Thomas Ewing, Kansas General

CONFLICTING STATEMENT:

"A camp of colored recruits ...was early warned by the Lieutenant in charge, and, with one exception, escaped to the woods in safety."

– James Winchell, Raid Survivor

ON THE SUMMIT

At 5 a.m. on Aug. 21, 1863, Quantrill halted his command on a summit southeast of Lawrence. The guerrillas discarded the Union uniforms they had been wearing to deceive Kansas troops. Quantrill was eager to know if he had caught the town by surprise or if the militia was waiting in ambush for him behind fortified positions. He knew his command would be annihilated if the town had been forewarned. To find out, Quantrill sent two guerrillas to reconnoiter. Resident Hovey Lowman saw the men and wrote,

COL JOSIAH MILLER.. DESCRIBED AS A CIVILIAN, HE WAS ACTUALLY A MEMBER OF THE GOVERNOR'S MILITARY STAFF. HIS BROTHER GEORGE MILLER WAS A MISSOURI MINISTER AND FRIEND OF QUANTRILL (FROM HISTORY OF LAWRENCE, KANSAS BY CORDLEY).

"Two horsemen [were] sent forward to reconnoiter the town. The men rode up and down Massachusetts Street from one end to the other and reported that the town was sleeping. [1]

While waiting for his scouts to return, Quantrill rode to the house of Josiah Miller at the base of the summit. Miller was Colonel and judge advocate on Kansas Governor Thomas Carney's military staff. Ironically, Josiah's brother, George Miller, was a pro-Southern Missouri minister and friend of Quantrill. The senior Miller was not home, but his son, William, a member of Company

---

1   Lowman, p. 44.

G, Kansas Militia, answered the door. Quantrill identified himself as a Union officer from Fort Scott on a forced march and wanted to know if Union troops were in town. William doubted his authenticity and replied no. Just then, his sister entered the room and recognized Quantrill. She blurted out, "You are not soldiers, you are Quantrill's." The chieftain replied, "You have guessed right, I am Quantrill."[2]

Quantrill then returned to the summit as a lone rider approached out of the dark. Wearing a Union uniform and armed with a shotgun, 16-year-old Hoffman Collamore, son of Lawrence mayor and militia Gen. George Collamore, had awakened early to hunt prairie chickens on his father's farm south of Lawrence. Observing that the guerrillas were wearing Union uniforms, Hoffman paid them little attention and began to pass. One guerrilla halted him and asked where he was going. Hoffman gave a nonchalant reply to which the guerrilla cursed and shot him. The bullet entered Hoffman's thigh, and he fell from his horse. Hoffman played dead and survived his wound.

The guerrillas then saw individuals riding south out of Lawrence. This group, consisting of young locals Steve Horton, Nin Beck, Sallie Young, and John Donnelley, was out for an early morning ride. Although texts portray the young men as civilians, Donnelley was, in fact, a private in the 11th Kansas Cavalry. Young admitted in her testimony she knew Donnelley was a Kansas soldier but thought he was a lieutenant. Several guerrillas rode after the group, but all escaped except Young. She was brought before Quantrill and ordered to identify individuals in town that were on their death lists.

Quantrill's scouts returned and reported the town sleeping. Quantrill called his lieutenants together and gave them specific assignments. The main column was to charge down Massachusetts Street while other detachments were to branch off on the parallel north-south streets of New Hampshire and Vermont. This maneuver was intended to prevent men from escaping out the back door of their homes and businesses. Quantrill also sent 11 men to the top

---

2   William Miller, "William Miller Reminiscences," (unpublished, 1913): 1-2 Kansas Collection, Lawrence, KS, University of Kansas, Kenneth Spencer Research Library.

SALLIE YOUNG – ACCUSED OF BEING A GUERRILLA SPY
(FROM BLOODY DAWN BY GOODRICH)

of Mount Oread to serve as lookouts. Before entering Lawrence, Quantrill turned to his men and said, "Boys, this is the home of Jim Lane and [Charles] Jennison; remember that in hunting us they gave no quarter. Shoot every soldier you see, but in no way harm a woman or child."[3] Guerrilla Andy Walker recalled, "Orders were to kill every man but to spare the women and boys."[4]

---

3   Barton, p. 125.

4   Eakin, p. 61.

At this critical moment, a group of guerrillas lost their courage and said they wanted to forego the attack and return to Missouri. A nonplussed Quantrill replied, "[He] was going in and they might follow who would."[5] He rode forward, and the command followed.

As they descended the summit, two guerrillas saw local S. S. Snyder milking a cow outside his barn near the Miller house. Snyder was minister for the German United Brethren Church and a lieutenant in the 2nd Kansas Colored Regiment. He became Lawrence's first victim.

ATTACK ON UNION CAMPS

As the raiders neared the downtown section, squads broke off and rode down their assigned streets. One witness described the guerrillas' approach: "On their first attack their columns had spread out like a fan, and with squads dashing at the top of their speed had within a few minutes taken possession of every quarter of the place."[6] The Rev. Cordley recalled the precision of their charge: "The attack was perfectly planned. Every man knew his place. Detachments scattered to every section of the town, and it was done with such promptness and speed that before people could gather the meaning of their first yell, every part of the town was full of them. They flowed into every street and lane like water dashed upon a rock."[7]

While the main column rode down Massachusetts Street, a squad veered off and attacked the 14th Kansas Cavalry where twenty-two recruits camped. Guerrilla Andy Walker recalled, "A detachment left the column when the soldiers' tents appeared and hurled itself into their camp. The recruits swarmed out all dazed in their night clothes. It was not long before they were all dead."[8] The guerrillas killed eighteen of the twenty-two soldiers.

---

5   Richard Cordley, *A History of Lawrence, Kansas*, p. 195.

6   R. G. Elliott, "The Quantrill Raid As Seen from the Eldridge House," *Kansas Collections, Kansas State Historical Society, Vol. 8*, p. 185.

7   J. S. Broughton, *The Lawrence Massacre By A Band of Missouri Ruffians Under Quantrill, August 21, 1863*, (Lawrence, KS: J. S. Broughton publisher, 1865), p. 3.

8   Eakin, p. 61.

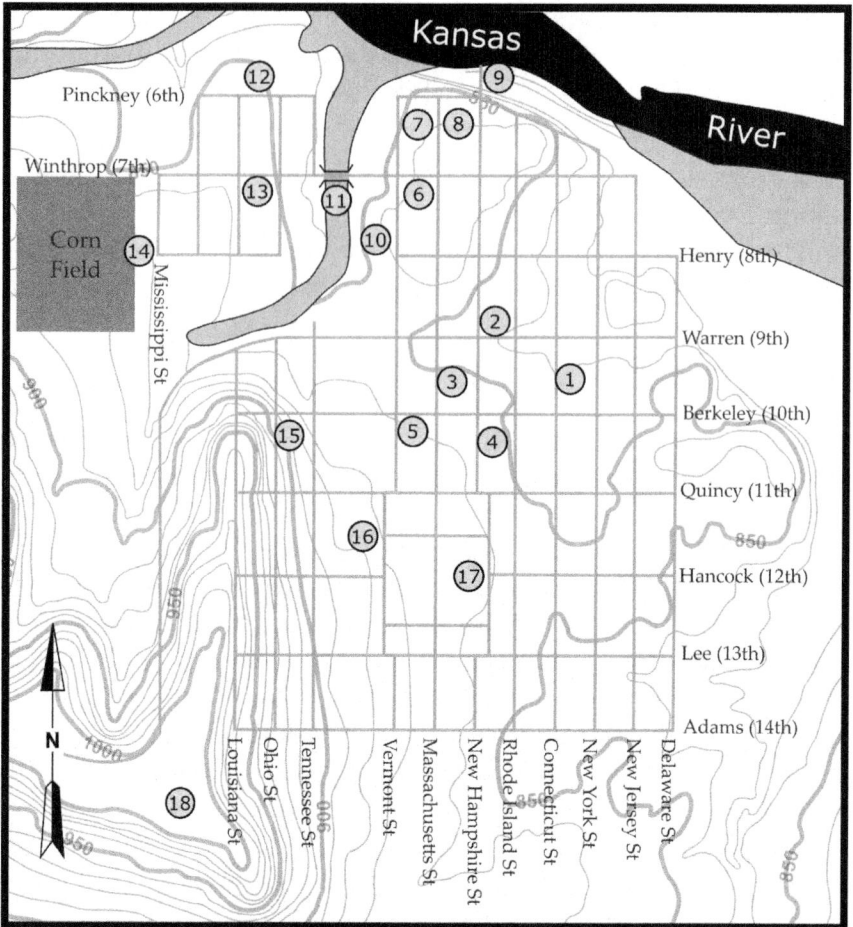

MAP OF DOWNTOWN LAWRENCE – AUGUST 21, 1863 (CIVILWARMUSE)

1. Ed Fitch House	10. Johnson House
2. Bullene House	11. Ravine dividing East and West Lawrence
3. 14th Kansas Cavalry Camp	12. Collamore House
4. Grosvenor house	13. Griswold, Thorpe, Baker and Trask Home
5. 2nd Kansas Colored Camp	14. Lane Home
6. Eldridge House	15. Bell House
7. Robinson House	16. Fisher House
8. Whitney House	17. South Park
9. Ferry	18. Mt. Oread Entrenchments

One of the bravest recruits was Pvt. James Cooper. Cooper had been a cadet at West Point and, upon graduation, was commissioned a second lieutenant in the prestigious 2nd United States Cavalry. He was initially stationed at Santa Fe, New Mexico, but when the war erupted, Cooper was assigned to the Army of the Potomac. Sadly, he was court-martialed for drunkenness and dismissed from the Army. Cooper still wanted to fight and traveled to Kansas, where he enlisted as a private in the 14th Kansas Cavalry.

On the morning of the raid, Cooper was standing guard armed with a musket and fixed bayonet. His comrade, Pvt. Cosma Colman, was also awake and heard Cooper's alert that the camp was under attack. Colman ran among the tents shouting, "Quantrill is here." Colman recalled that he and fellow soldiers Jim Cooper, Charley Allen, Sam Markham, and a Holloway boy tried to escape. They were all killed except for Colman after they'd run a short distance.

Private Cooper, however, went down fighting. After retreating a few steps, he stopped and cried out, "Damned if I run another inch." Cooper faced his pursuers and lowered his musket at 'charge bayonet' position. After the raid, he was found with four bullets in his chest.[9] Pvt. James Cooper sacrificed his life defending the town and is one of Lawrence's unsung heroes.

RECRUITS OF THE 14TH KANSAS CAVALRY

The murder of the young, unarmed 14th Kansas Cavalry recruits has been used by survivors and historians as propaganda to demonstrate the guerrillas' brutality. John Speer, whose son was a member of the 14th Kansas Cavalry and killed in the raid, wrote, "[The 14th Kansas Cavalry] were not soldiers, having no drill as soldiers. They were boys so young that it was a common remark that Captain [Leroy] Beam was gathering in all the infants — boys so young they were considered as infants unfit for service. They

---

9   Sheridan, Colman, "The Massacre of Union Cavalry Recruits," pp. 199-202.

JOHN SPEER – FORMER JAYHAWKER AND SUPPORTER OF SENATOR JIM LANE.
OWNED KANSAS TRIBUNE NEWSPAPER. TWO OF HIS BOYS WERE KILLED DURING RAID.
(FROM LIFE OF JAMES H. LANE BY SPEER)

were called 'Beam's Babes.'"[10] But Speer's statement is false. Kansas historian Richard Sheridan found that the recruits ages ranged from 16 to 36; the median age being 18, and the average 21.[11]

Speer also fails to acknowledge the ages of Quantrill's men. Survivor Laura Anderson indicated the guerrillas she encountered were between 16 and 20. A small sample of guerrillas known to be present during the raid reflects the following ages: Plunk Murry (16), Allen Parmer (15), Frank Smith (17), Archie Clement (17), William

---

10   Sheridan, John Speer, "Statement of John Speer," p. 325.

11   *Ibid.*

Gaugh (17), Columbus C. Haynes (17) Samuel Hilton (16), Morgan Mattox (17), James Mundy (17), James Barnett (17), Sam Constable (16), Riley Crawford (15), James O. Hinde (17) and John Prewitt (16). The facts suggest that boys were fighting boys.

Quantrill's Attack On The 2nd Kansas Colored Regiment

While the 14th Kansas Cavalry soldiers were being overrun, the 2nd Kansas Colored Regiment camp, located on the southwest corner of Massachusetts and Berkley Street, was also being attacked. Historians have never determined how many black soldiers died in the engagement. General Thomas Ewing believed at least 20 were killed. Still, Lawrence local James Winchell said, "A camp

Photo taken from the Mt. Oread entrenchments in 1867
- by Alexander Gardner — (Library of Congress)

of colored recruits, I am told, located in the southern suburb, was early warned by the lieutenant in charge and, with one exception, escaped to the woods in safety."[12]

Winchell's statement agrees with the account of black survivor Andrew Williams. Williams said that very few if any, black soldiers were killed. Williams recalled that as soon as he heard gunfire, he hid among the dense foliage along the Kansas River. He wrote, "About half the colored recruits were there, having run at the sound of the first pistol and the sight of [William] Gregg's party firing on the white [14th Kansas Cavalry] camp."[13]

With the soldiers cast aside, the guerrillas unleashed their fury on Lawrence.

12   *The New York Times,* Aug. 31, 1863.

13   Connelley, Quantrill and the Border Wars, p. 337n.

CHAPTER 9

THE SURRENDER OF LAWRENCE

POPULAR VERSION:

> "... an onslaught was made on the Johnson House, and though no red legs were known to be in town, and certainly none fell victims ..."

> —R. G. Elliott, Raid Survivor

CONFLICTING STATEMENT:

> "Members of the celebrated 'Red Legs' still reside here and individual members were hunted on the morning of the raid with unusual care and perseverance."

> —H. S. Clarke, Raid Survivor

THE GUERRILLAS CHARGE DOWN MASSACHUSETTS STREET

Having attacked the 14th Kansas Cavalry and 2nd Kansas Colored soldiers, the main command of Quantrill's force charged up Massachusetts Street in columns of four. Cordley described the scene: "The horsemanship of the guerrillas was perfect. They rode with that ease and abandon which are acquired only by a life spent in

LOOKING NORTH ON MASSACHUSETTS STREET – NOTICE WIDTH OF STREET.
(FROM BLOODY DAWN BY GOODRICH)

the saddle amid desperate scenes. Their horses scarcely seemed to touch the ground, and the riders sat with bodies and arms perfectly free, with revolvers on full cock, shooting at every house and man they passed, and yelling like demons at every bound."[1]

Since Cordley describes the guerrillas as 'shooting at every man they saw,' who were the men out on Massachusetts Street at 5 a.m.? Historian Richard Sheridan says many business owners, or their hired help, were sleeping in their stores. He concluded that when they heard firing, they came out to see what was happening and found themselves in harm's way.

But storekeepers were not the only ones in the street; many were soldiers and militiamen. Witness testimony indicates that many 14th Kansas recruits were sleeping outside on a plank sidewalk rather than their tents because of the heat. One local confirmed, "Several new recruits were sleeping on the plank sidewalk in front of their quarters on account of the heat of the weather and were

---

1   Cordley, A History of Lawrence, Kansas: From the Earliest Settlement to the Close of the Rebellion, p. 196.

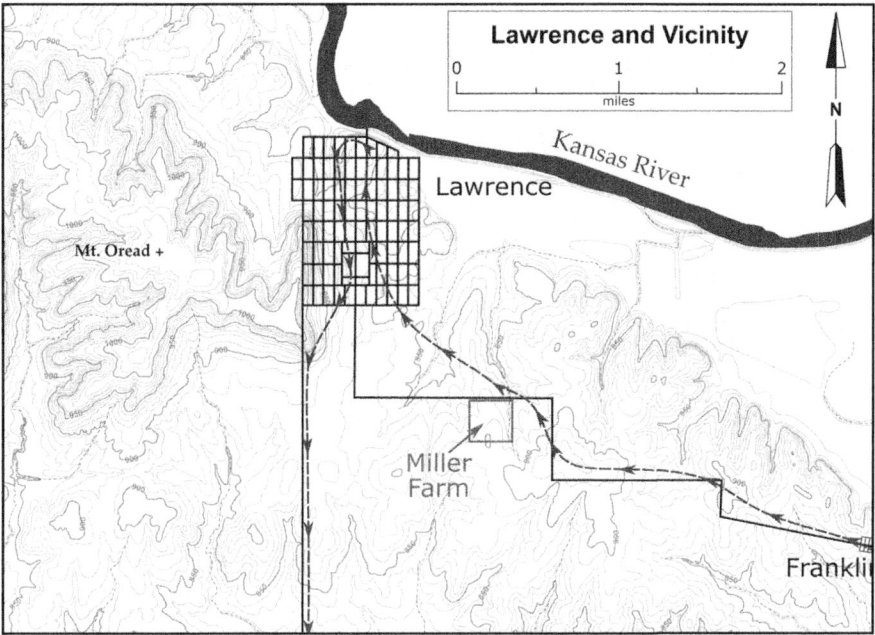

PATH OF GUERRILLA ENTRANCE AND EXIT OF LAWRENCE - (CIVILWARMUSE).

shot as they lay when the gang first entered."[2] There was also a Union Army recruiting station located near the intersection of Massachusetts and Henry (8th) streets. A source said when the officers saw the guerrillas, they ran into the street. Militiamen were also running down Massachusetts Street to grab their weapons at the armory. One of them, Lieutenant Fred Kimball, was carrying the keys to the arsenal and was on his way to unlock the door. His comrade, Sergeant E. R. Falley found Kimball in the street shot to pieces short of his destination.[3] Kansas Col. John Rankin saw a militiaman in the street: "This man had undoubtedly belonged to the militia and had his accouterments on and gun in his hand but he made no effort to shoot or resist."[4]

---

2   Sheridan, Winchell, Statement of J. M. Winchell, p. 182.

3   David Dary, *Lawrence, Douglas County, Kansas, An Informal History* (Lawrence, KS: Allen Books, 1982), p. 106.

4   Connelley Collection, Statement of John K. Rankin.

COL. JOHN K. RANKIN –
(FROM HISTORY OF LAWRENCE,
KANSAS *BY CORDLEY)*

ROBERT G. ELLIOT – RAID SURVIVOR
(FROM HISTORY OF LAWRENCE,
KANSAS *BY CORDLEY)*

Quantrill's attack was so unexpected the militia had no time to organize a defense. One survivor admitted, "Even if the company could have got together, they had no arms and there could be no resistance from the houses themselves...The attack was so sudden and the occupation of the town was so complete, that no general rally was possible."[5] Survivor R. G. Elliott agreed, saying "as [local militia] ran out to either form in companies or to find a place of security — they were shot down as some many wolves."[6] Witness Erastus Ladd believed the guerrillas shot the men in the streets "... in order to prevent any concentration or organization on our part for a defense."[7]

---

5   Cordley, A History of Lawrence, Kansas, pp. 199-200.

6   Letter from R. G. Elliott to Dear Sister, Aug. 24, 1863, "Letters from Robert Gaston Elliott" by Carolyn Berneking, *The Kansas Historical Quarterly*, Autumn 1977 (Vol. 43, No. 3), www.kshs.org/p/a-look-at-early-lawrence/13271

7   Russell E. Bidlack, "Erastus D. Ladd's Description of the Lawrence Massacre," *The Kansas Historical Quarterly,* Summer 1963, (Vol. 29, No. 2), pp. 113-121. www.kshs.org/publicat/khq/1963/1963summer_bidlack.pdf

SKETCH OF FERRY OVER THE KANSAS RIVER IN 1857 LAWRENCE –
(FROM BEYOND THE MISSISSIPPI BY RICHARDSON)

As the guerrillas neared the north end of Massachusetts Street, they rode past the Eldridge House Hotel and went directly to the ferry that crossed the Kansas River. Quantrill was aware that 12 soldiers of the 12th Kansas Infantry were camped on the north side of the river, and he wanted to prevent them from crossing over. Quantrill sent 15 guerrillas down to the ferry to skirmish with them while he continued his attack. To the credit of these Kansas sharpshooters, their brisk fire kept the guerrillas away from the northern part of town.

SURRENDER OF THE ELDRIDGE HOUSE

Having secured the ferry, the guerrillas circled back to the Eldridge House and surrounded it. The hotel, rebuilt after Missourians burned it to the ground in 1856, was a four-story brick dwelling with protective iron grilles covering the ground-floor windows.

ELDRIDGE HOUSE HOTEL – (BLOODY DAWN BY GOODRICH)

At the time of the raid, there were 60 guests inside the Eldridge House. One or two were out-of-state businessmen, while the rest were residents or locals who had attended a railroad meeting at the hotel on the night of August 20th. Because the business session had lasted until after midnight, many decided to spend the night.

The guerrillas prepared to charge the hotel's main entrance, as they believed soldiers would be inside defending the building. Quantrill was pleasantly surprised when Kansas provost marshal Capt. Alexander Banks hung a white bed sheet out a second-story window and signaled the surrender of the hotel. Banks summoned Quantrill and asked, "What is your object in coming to Lawrence?" Quantrill replied, "Plunder." Banks responded, "We are defenseless and at your mercy, the house is surrendered, but we demand protection for the inmates."[8] Quantrill agreed to his terms and

---

8   Connelley, Quantrill and the Border Wars, p. 342n-343n.

saved the lives of 60 men. In a short time, Quantrill's promise to protect his prisoners would be tested as he would risk his life to ensure their safety.

As the guerrillas entered the hotel, a gong rang out. The attackers backed outside thinking they were walking into an ambush. But when no shots were fired, the guerrillas re-entered the lobby with pistols drawn.

While the guests were assembling in the lobby under guard, guerrillas were going door to door to ensure they had all presented themselves. One or two resisted demands to leave their rooms but were quickly overpowered and sent downstairs. As the guests descended the stairs, they came to a landing where two raiders relieved them of weapons, money, and jewelry. One guest, Judge Lawrence Bailey, said that although he resented being robbed, he appreciated the fact that the guerrillas were polite and took his possessions without search or rudeness. He wrote, "No violence was used and no loud or boisterous talk was indulged in."[9]

Sorties to the homes of Gen. George Collamore, Senator Jim Lane, the Johnson House, and City Magazine

With the surrender of the Eldridge House, the threat of resistance was alleviated. Quantrill ordered his men "to first set fire to the Eldridge House and all the houses on Main (Massachusetts Street), then scatter over the town and set fire to houses as they went ... for them not to go into any part of the town where the people were firing guns, as they had to hurry away and had not time to engage with the scattered persons at their houses."[10]

One witness noted the guerrillas' discipline and wrote, "It did not seem necessary for the captains to issue them orders; everyone, apparently, knew what he was to do. The men quickly formed into three main units; one, whose area of operation was to be Massachusetts Street, a second assigned to the territory west of

---

9   Lawrence D. Bailey, "A Graphic Description of the Quantrill Raid on Lawrence, Kansas" *The Kansas Cultivator*, 1887, p. 8.

10   Cone, Roenigk (ed), p. 9.

Massachusetts, and a third to the eastern section of the town."[11] Accordingly, Quantrill assigned the east side of Lawrence to Colonel John Holt's Confederate recruits; the west side to Bill Anderson's Jackson County men, and the rest to Massachusetts Street.

Four sorties were carried out in tandem. The first was directed at the house of Gen. George Collamore, located on the west side of town. The guerrillas did not want to give him time to organize a defense. Collamore saw the guerrillas approaching and, with his aide, Pat Keefe, hid in a well adjacent to his house. The guerrillas were unable to find Collamore and set his home on fire. The billowing smoke resulted in both men dying from asphyxiation.

Local Arthur Spicer, former Free State Militiaman and Stubbs Rifle member led a second sortie. Spicer knew Quantrill from earlier days, and when the attack occurred, he made his way to the Eldridge House. Quantrill saw him and asked if his brother, Col. Newell Spicer, 1st Kansas Cavalry, was in town. Arthur replied he was at Fort Smith, Arkansas. However, one account suggests Newell was present as he signed a commemorative book vouching he was a survivor. Quantrill told Spicer to escort one of his squads to the ammunition depot so it could be destroyed. Spicer failed to find the depot because it was frequently moved from one building to another. One frustrated guerrilla was about to shoot Spicer when George Todd appeared and saved his life. Todd escorted Spicer to the Whitney House, and he survived the raid. Surprisingly, this would not be the only life Todd would save during the raid.

THE JOHNSON HOUSE AND THE EXISTENCE OF RED LEGS IN LAWRENCE

A third sortie focused on the Johnson House. This hotel was the headquarters for the Red Legs paramilitary organization. One source corroborated, "The Johnson House, second in accommodations to the Eldridge House, was known as the stopping place of the Red

---

11 Allen Crafton, *Free State Fortress: The First Ten Years of the History of Lawrence,* Kansas (Lawrence, KS: The World Company, 1954), p. 190.

RALPH DIX – DIX WAS CAPTURED INSIDE THE JOHNSON HOUSE (RED LEG HEADQUARTERS) AND EXECUTED. (FROM HISTORY OF LAWRENCE, KANSAS BY CORDLEY)

Legs."[12] The guerrillas knew that many Lawrence men were Red Leg members. One historian confirmed, "Lawrence also contributed a disproportionate number of its men to the quasi-military organization

---

12 Elliott, "The Quantrill Raid As Seen from the Eldridge House," p. 193.

of scouts known as Red Legs."[13] The guerrillas treated every man captured at the hotel as a Red Leg. They walked the prisoners across the street into an alley and shot them down in cold blood.

Ralph Dix's home was next to the Johnson House, making him a suspected Red Leg. A native from Connecticut, Dix had earlier worked for the Colt Rifle Company, which cast further suspicion about his involvement in military affairs. Dix was inside the Johnson House when the guerrillas attacked. His wife, seeing the town overrun, begged him to hide. But Dix declined and said, "No, I want to await developments and aid the citizens. Our arms are across the street in the arsenal and surely some resistance will be made."[14] Another survivor added, "[Dix's] (militia?) company like others were defenseless, having returned their guns to the armory."[15] Dix and his company surrendered and were executed.

It comes as no surprise that survivor testimony avoids admitting the presence of Red Legs in Lawrence. Locals knew they could not claim to be helpless if they were known to be in town. To convince the public of their innocence, R. G. Elliott wrote, "An onslaught was made on the Johnson House ... though no red legs were known to be in town, and certainly none fell victims."[16]

But H. S. Clarke's recollection conflicts with Elliott's. Clarke wrote, "Members of the celebrated 'Red Legs' still reside here and individual members were hunted on the morning of the raid with unusual care and perseverance."[17] One local confirmed that "they [Red Legs] were cordially hated by the Quantrill party, and individual members were hunted on the morning of the raid with unusual care and perseverance."[18] The fact that Red Legs resided in Lawrence is further corroborated by H. B. Leonard,

---

13 Sheridan, Colman, "The Massacre of Union Cavalry Recruits," p. 324.

14 *Lawrence Journal World,* "Lawrence Today and Yesterday, Semi-Centennial Memorial," August 21, 1913.

15 *Ibid.*

16 Elliott, p. 194.

17 John C. Shea, *Reminiscences of Quantrell's Raid upon the City of Lawrence, Kansas,* (Kansas City, Mo.: I. P. Moore, Printer, 1879), p. 9.

18 *Ibid.,* p. 9.

JOHN L. CRANE – MILITIAMAN CAPTURED AND KILLED AT JOHNSON HOUSE
(FROM HISTORY OF LAWRENCE, KANSAS BY CORDLEY)

who recalled that known Red Leg members Capt. Bloom Swain, Wash Buchanan, George Hunter, and John Eldridge were in town the day of the attack.[19]

Lt. Nimrod Hankins of the 9th Kansas Cavalry (stationed at Shawneetown, Kansas) also gave evidence of Red Legs living in Lawrence. A few months before the raid, Hankins wrote his commander, "There was about fifty Red Legs passed here Saturday evening going home to Lawrence. All leading horses (from Missouri)."[20]

---

19 Connelley Collection, Statement of H. B. Leonard.

20 Missouri's Union Provost Marshal Papers: 1861-1866. Jefferson City, MO, Missouri State Archives.

A few guerrillas identified men they claimed to be Red Legs. One guerrilla recognized an Eldridge House prisoner as a Red Leg and attempted to kill him. He was prevented from doing so by a guard who stated the man was under Quantrill's protection. Another guerrilla bragged to his comrades, "I have killed seven 'red legs' and I'll kill eight more."[21]

In another incident, two more suspected Red Legs were taken prisoner. George Holt and John Crane (a militia member), lived near the Johnson House and were known radical abolitionists. As they were being led to the Eldridge Hotel, a passing guerrilla recognized them and said Holt and Crane "had been in Missouri killing our people."[22] They were immediately executed. In the final analysis, readers should remember that aside from locals who identified Red Legs, no one can prove or disprove who was or wasn't a Red Leg as no official roster was ever made of the secret organization.

QUANTRILL AT THE HOME OF JIM LANE

Jacob Rote led the fourth sortie. He took Quantrill and a squad of guerrillas to the home of Jim Lane, located on the west side of town. Lane had earlier heard the guerrillas attacking and found shelter in a cornfield behind his house. Mrs. Mary Lane greeted the guerrilla chief at the door, and he asked if her husband was home. She replied he was away on business. Quantrill tipped his hat and said, "Give the general [my] compliments," and added he hoped they would meet one day. Mrs. Lane replied, "Mr. Lane would be very glad to meet him under different circumstances."[23] Quantrill told Mrs. Lane that her house was to be burned and, out of courtesy, left a detachment of men to help her remove furniture — an extremely magnanimous and unprecedented gesture.

---

21 *Lawrence Journal World,* "Today and Yesterday."

22 Lowman, p. 80.

23 Cordley, *A History of Lawrence, Kansas,* p. 220.

QUANTRILL RETURNS TO THE ELDRIDGE HOUSE

Having failed to capture Lane, Quantrill returned to the Eldridge House, where a witness recalled, "To some acquaintances he (Quantrill) spoke civilly enough, and with two or three shook hands...[He said] that [the guests] were entirely safe, and should receive complete protection from personal violence."[24] Quantrill also assured the women they would not be subjected to sexual abuse, adding that Lane's Jayhawkers did not share this courtesy with Missouri women. One guest asked him if the hotel was going to be burned, to which he replied, "Yes, it will be burnt... We have had our houses burnt and we will burn also."[25] Another prisoner asked why the guerrillas had not attacked the week before, and Quantrill replied, "You were expecting me then — but I have caught you napping now."[26]

With his prisoners safe inside the hotel, Quantrill rode over to the Whitney House. This hotel was located next to the Kansas River and within musket range of the soldiers stationed across the river. Mrs. Addie Stewart Graton, whose husband was a Union officer, saw Quantrill ride over and recalled, "A horseman came at full speed up New Hampshire Street from Winthrop. When within a few yards of the [Whitney] house, there was a sharp report of a rifle from over the river. The man instantly flung himself upon the opposite side of his horse and clung to his neck. ... The rider rushed on at such a furious pace that I thought he would not be able to stop before he was on me, but, checking his horse so suddenly that he sat back on his haunches, at the edge of the porch, the rider dismounted, tied the bridle to a porch post and then stalked past into the house. The man was Quantrill."[27] Quantrill made his headquarters at the hotel, and the Stone family prepared him a breakfast.

---

24 Sheridan, R. G. Elliott, "The Quantrill Raid As Seen From the Eldridge House," p. 175.

25 Bailey, p. 9.

26 Cordley, "Quantrill's Raid or The Lawrence Massacre: August 21, 1863," p. 2.

27 Betty Laird, "Quantrill Raid – A Compilation of Articles, Letters and Other Material from the Watkins Museum Archives," Lawrence, KS, Watkins Museum, August 1988.

Conflict Back At The Eldridge House

As soon as Quantrill left the Eldridge House, many guests became concerned for their safety. Their worst fears were confirmed when a guerrilla entered and shouted, "Now, we will shoot the men." Fortunately, one of Quantrill's guards replied, "No, we are not to shoot these men. It is against orders." The antagonist continued to threaten the prisoners, to which the guard threatened, "If you shoot any of these men, I will shoot you."[28] To his credit, this guerrilla saved the lives of 60 men.

Guerrilla Larkin Skaggs created another problem. Skaggs, a Baptist minister from Cass County, Missouri, was robbing guests in the lobby when he ordered Miss Lydia Stone, whose father owned the Whitney House, to give him a ring she was wearing. Skaggs was unaware that Quantrill had given this ring to Lydia years earlier in gratitude for her nursing him back to health after he fell ill living at the Whitney House. Lydia gave Skaggs the ring and begged a guard to fetch Quantrill. When Quantrill returned, Lydia told him what happened, and he promised the ring would be returned. Quantrill found Skaggs and made him give the ring back. Before leaving, a humiliated Skaggs turned to Lydia and said she would be sorry. Quantrill then returned to the Whitney House.

This encounter between Quantrill and Lydia at the Eldridge House raises questions. The two obviously knew each other but acted as if they were strangers. Lydia was a beautiful lady, but there is no evidence that the two were intimate. The Stone family obviously supported Quantrill and most likely provided him with information about the town. However, Lydia had no reason to be at the Eldridge House at 5 a.m., given that her father owned a competing hotel — the Whitney House — one block away.

There exists another version of this incident that makes more sense. Survivor Loring J. Oldham places the event not at the Eldridge House, but the Whitney House, which was owned by Nathan Stone, Lydia's father. Oldham said that after the Eldridge House surrendered, Quantrill went to the Whitney House, where Lydia prepared a breakfast. When Lydia stepped out on the porch,

---

28   Griffith, p. 134.

LYDIA STONE – QUANTRILL'S FRIEND. (FROM BLOODY DAWN BY GOODRICH)

WHITNEY HOUSE – WHERE ELDRIDGE HOUSE PRISONERS STAYED.
(FROM QUANTRILL AND THE BORDER WARS BY CONNELLEY)

Larkin Skaggs rode by and ordered her to give him the ring. Lydia subsequently cried for Quantrill, who rose from the table and demanded Skaggs return the ring.[29]

Back at the Eldridge House, local attorney Robert S. Stevens was concerned for his safety and the safety of others. Stevens noticed flames coming from the basement and knew that a pharmacy was located there. He was afraid the fire might cause the chemicals to explode and kill everyone inside. Stevens pleaded for a guard to bring Quantrill back to the hotel. When the chieftain returned a second time, Stevens flashed Masonic signs of distress at him. The two men talked privately, and at the end of their discussion, Quantrill told the prisoners, "All of you go over to the City Hotel [the Whitney House], and go into it, and stay in it, and you will be safe. But don't attempt to go into the streets."[30]

---

29 Connelley Collection, Statement of Loring J. Oldham.

30 James M. Winchell, *The New York Daily Times,* Aug. 31, 1863.

Like his encounter with Lydia Stone, this episode between Quantrill and Stevens is suspicious. It's believed both men knew each other but acted like strangers. Evidence suggests that years earlier, Stevens represented Quantrill in court on charges of horse stealing. Judge Lawrence Bailey recalled, "Robert S. Stevens, formerly a partner with (pro-Southern) Gov. Shannon at Lecompton, had come the night before and had been acquainted with Quantrell [sic], I think, in his legal character, perhaps in assisting him out of some scrape. I was also told that he [Stevens] was a Mason and knew Quantrill to be one and that he made use of Masonic signs to attract attention."[31] Sara T. Robinson added: "He (Quantrill) had employed Robert S. Stevens of Lecompton, when arrested for horse stealing, and won the case."[32]

When Quantrill ordered the hotel to be evacuated, the guests were taken outside and placed in a circular earthwork. Precisely what this structure was is debatable. Again, we need to remember that survivors wanted to downplay the fact that Lawrence had defensive fortifications. One prisoner described it as an 'old circus ring,' while another said it was an old 1856 entrenchment whose walls had eroded from the weather. [33] However, Pvt. Colman identified the structure as an active defensive fortification built by the militia.

The guerrillas dismissed the women, and the guards began marching their prisoners toward the Whitney House. One soldier, Union Maj. F. B. Bancroft, 8th Kansas Infantry, was staying at the hotel while recuperating from an illness he contracted at Vicksburg, Mississippi. He was so weak his friends had to carry him while he sat in an armchair. Bancroft saw Larkin Skaggs dragging an American flag in the dirt and shouted, "There, they are dragging the American Flag in the dust, God damn them."[34] To avoid coming under fire from the soldiers across the river, the prisoners were escorted east on Winthrop Street and then north on New Hampshire to the Whitney House.

---

31 L. D. Bailey and others, *Quantrill's Raid on Lawrence*, (Lyndon, KS: 1899), p. 8.

32 Sheridan, Robinson, "The Governor's Wife Recalls the Raid," p. 208.

33 *The New York Daily Tribune*, Aug. 31, 1863.

34 Shea, p. 21.

During the march, two incidents occurred that might have led to a disaster. One guerrilla rode up to a prisoner and shouted, "God damn you! You are a Red Leg!"[35]and fired but missed his intended victim. Before he could shoot again, George Todd rode over and ordered him to stop. The guerrilla argued the man was a Red Leg and his orders were to kill every one of them. Todd replied the man was under Quantrill's protection and that he would shoot the guerrilla if he fired again.

Prisoner R. G. Elliott recalled another incident. He said that a group of guerrillas, described as a "loose gang," suddenly dashed up and announced they would kill the prisoners. Guerrilla David Porter stood between the gang and his prisoners. When Porter told them they were under Quantrill's protection, one attacker replied, "Damn you, I won't obey you, and I will shoot Quantrill myself." Porter stood his ground and said, "I am placed here to protect these prisoners, and I will do it. If you shoot any of them, I will kill you."[36]

During this exchange, a second guard saw Quantrill outside the Whitney House and called him over. Elliott said that as soon as he arrived, "[Quantrill] was met with a clash of demands, the [guerrilla] guard demanding to know if he had not given orders for the protection of the prisoners and the [loose gang] clamored to attack them." Quantrill told the loose gang "That as [the prisoners] had surrendered he had pledged them protection, and with a tone and imprecation that quelled opposition, he swore that he would do it if he had to kill every man who interfered."[37] The actions of Porter and Quantrill resulted in the lives of 60 Lawrence men being saved for the third time.

The prisoners arrived at the Whitney House and were instructed to go inside and stay there until the raid was over. To ensure their safety, Quantrill had his own men guard the hotel to prevent others from entering. One prisoner understood Quantrill's thinking and said, "Sentries were posted in front of [Whitney House], as I

---

35 *The New York Times*, Aug. 31, 1863.

36 Sheridan, R. S. Stevens, "Protecting the Prisoners at the Eldridge House," p. 170.

37 Elliott, p. 190.

G. W. E. GRIFFITH – MILITIAMAN IMPRISONED AT WHITNEY HOUSE.
(FROM MY 96 YEARS IN THE GREAT WEST BY GRIFFITH)

supposed, to keep us in; but I afterwards concluded that it was for our protection, and to keep the drunken and violent members of the gang from molesting us."[38]

It wasn't long before the prisoners discovered they had another problem. The soldiers across the river were unaware they were inside the Whitney House and continued to fire at the hotel. Fearing an errant shot would kill someone, the prisoners asked for a volunteer to go down to the river and tell the soldiers

---

38   Sheridan, L. D. Bailey, "Recollections of the Raid." p. 191.

to stop firing. When no one stepped forward, Lydia Stone ran to the river waving a white handkerchief and succeeded in having the soldiers cease fire.

It's interesting to note that after the raid several survivors developed bitter resentments against the Whitney House prisoners and accused them of being Southern sympathizers. One complained, "[The guerrillas] killed everything they saw except a few persons at the Whitney House, a few copperheads (Southern sympathizers)."[39] Prisoner G. W. E. Griffith studied his fellow captees and wrote, "I realized the fact that most of these were guests of the hotel and not residents of the city and that some of them were from the South."[40]

Survivors point to Hugh Walsh as an example of Southern sympathizers being held at the Whitney House. During the 'Bleeding Kansas' years, Walsh served as secretary to the pro-Southern Territorial Gov. James W. Denver and was once interim governor of the territory. One local said of Walsh, "He was a well-known proslavery man and had worked for making of Kansas a slave state."[41]

Walsh was also an enemy to Jayhawker and Red Leg members like Jim Lane, Charles Jennison, and James Montgomery. Indeed, in 1856, Walsh indicted Montgomery for destroying ballot boxes in Linn County, Kansas. One Whitney House prisoner said Walsh's behavior was suspicious: "[Walsh] was smoking a pipe with [Judge Lawrence] Bailey during the raid and said the raid had been provoked and brought on by depredations of the abolitionists called red legs who had for years made Lawrence their headquarters while enticing Negroes to run away from their masters and steal their horses or mules...He also spoke of the atrocious doings of some of the Kansas troops in the border counties of Missouri and burning of the town of Osceola."[42]

---

39 Ralph A. Monaco, Scattered to the Four Winds: General Order No. 11 and Martial Law in Jackson County, MO, 1863, (Kansas City, Mo.: Monaco Publishing, LLC, 2014) p. 116.

40 Griffith, pp. 133, 134.

41 *Ibid.*, p. 135.

42 Bailey, p. 14.

It wasn't long before rumors of collusion between Whitney House prisoners and Quantrill spread all over town. Locals became more agitated when they learned that Quantrill had friendly discussions with suspected copperheads and Masons. These men included Ansom Storm, Captain F. B. Swift, Thomas Sternberg, James Christian, and W. H. R. Lykins.[43] Christian and Lykins were both anti-Lane leaders, and Lykins was known to harbor pro-Southern sympathies.

In the final analysis, no one can deny the prisoners owed their lives to Quantrill. Yet, only two expressed their gratitude; one wrote, "[Quantrill and his guerrillas] not only promised protection but were as good as their word."[44] Another said, "This protection [of prisoners], I think, [Quantrill] in all his power tried to redeem."[45]

FALSE ACCOUNTS REGARDING INCIDENTS AT THE ELDRIDGE HOUSE HOTEL

After the raid, survivors began to invent false stories about the events at the Eldridge House. One said, "[The guerrillas] set fire to the hotel. Then as the building burned and the people in the hotel attempted to leave it, they shot them down as fast as they came out."[46] Another accused the guerrillas of killing women and children inside the hotel; "In the Eldridge House I am informed that 15 women and children were burned to death."[47] Survivor Julia Louisa Lovejoy, whose husband was a chaplain in the 7th Kansas Cavalry, [a.k.a. Jennison's Jayhawkers], added to the misinformation: "There were a great many guests and boarders in the [Eldridge House], and as they rushed out they shot them down, and threw

---

43 *Lawrence Daily Journal,* Aug. 21, 1908.

44 Richard Cordley, "Quantrill's Raid or The Lawrence Massacre: August 21, 1863," Reproduced for the 125th Anniversary of Quantrill's Raid on Lawrence, Kansas, p. 6.

45 Sheridan, Winchell, "The Sacking of Lawrence," p. 185.

46 Letter from Alex Case to Dear Sir, Feb. 4, 1915, KSHS, Topeka, KS.

47 Letter from Samuel R. Ayres to Lyman Langdon, Aug. 24-27, 1863, KSHS, Topeka, KS.

their bodies back in to the fire."[48] Another source wrote, "A number of U. S. officers were called out of the hotels and as they made their appearance, sans culottes, an unceremonious bullet took them off without benefit of clergy or court martial."[49]

None of these claims are true. Indeed, not one Eldridge House guest was killed. However, one Ohio businessman was wounded when he refused to open the door to his room for a guerrilla. Unfortunately, these spurious allegations would not be the only ones written about the guerrillas.

The version of the raid historians want us to believe is false and full of many inconvenient truths that prove it wrong. The fact that many Lawrence men were members of the Red Legs, and Quantrill's protection of his prisoners are not welcome facts that survivors want the public to be aware of. In addition, the lies made up regarding the guerrilla treatment of their Eldridge House prisoners, like being thrown back into the fiery hotel, are nothing more than Northern propaganda.

---

48 Connelley Collection, Letter of Julia Louisa Lovejoy, August 22, 1863.

49 Banasik, p. 24.

CHAPTER 10

ACTS OF COMPASSION

POPULAR VERSION:

> "...they first shot every lady that they could find in the streets."

> – George Young, Raid Survivor

CONFLICTING STATEMENT:

> "The women were not insulted as has been represented."

> – Mrs. Elizabeth Earl, Raid Survivor

GUERRILLA BEHAVIOR

The popular version of the raid creates the illusion that Quantrill's entire guerrilla command was involved in the killings. However, evidence suggests that the men from Jackson County, Missouri, did most of the killing while others immersed themselves in less violent activities. Survivor Abigail Prentice Barber commented about the two entities "[Some guerrillas were] determined to kill every free state man and to wipe Lawrence from the map. Others were farmers whom Quantrill had compelled to join his forces. They were easily convinced they had not found the 'right man.' They were fed and treated hospitable and went away satisfied. There was no anger in their hearts."[1] Another survivor concurred with Barber, "It was noticed by many that the raiders were made up of mixed elements. Some came for plunder alone, others to burn and plunder, others to kill and destroy whatever came within reach, while a few, a very few, mixed with the crowd to save [lives]."[2] Reverend Cordley added, "The guerrillas differed very much in their spirit and conduct. Some of them were as humane as they could be in the work they were ordered to do. In some instances they advised men to get out of the way. They burned houses but were not unnecessarily harsh. They said they were obeying orders and doing a work that they hated and sometimes helped to save some of the furniture and things especially prized in houses they burned...They helped women take up the carpets and throw them out."[3]

In fact, several guerrillas told locals they had no idea that any killing would occur. Survivor H. S. Clarke recalled two guerrillas showing him their revolvers and saying they had not fired a shot all day and didn't intend to; that they had come to burn Lawrence, but not to kill. Another guerrilla said he thought the raid was supposed to re-capture some horses and that he hadn't killed anyone and wasn't going to. One other guerrilla told Mrs. Grosvenor, "...he had killed no one-did not intend to kill anyone [and] only taken some shirts and tobacco."[4] Survivor G. W. E. Griffith added, "Many of the men whom I met in the store talked freely with me and said they came to raid and burn the city in retaliation of the same thing done to them in Missouri and expressed their sorrow for innocent sufferers."[5] In addition, Castel said that Col. John Holt's 100 Confederate recruits dismounted on the east side of town and sat until told it was time to leave.[6]

---

1   Emporia State University, *News and Events Archive,* www.emporia.edu/news/archives/2001/jul2001/sam1.

2   Shea, p. 9.

3   Richard Cordley, *Pioneer Days in Kansas*, (Boston, Mass.: The Pilgrim Press, 1903), p. 209.

4   Connelley Collection, Statement of Mrs. Henry P. Grosvenor.

5   Sheridan, "Editor's Commentary," p. 315.

6   Castel, p. 295.

How Guerrillas Dealt With Women And Children

Some survivors falsely accused guerrillas of killing women and children. Local George Young said when the guerrillas attacked, "They first shot every lady that they could find in the streets."[7] Kansan Samuel R. Ayres overheard that, "In the Eldridge House I am informed that 15 women and children were burned to death."[8] Private Hervey Johnson of the 11th Kansas Cavalry wrote, "Men, women, and children were murdered without discrimination."[9] Albert Greene added that "every man, woman and child in town is dead."[10] Survivor Julia Louisa Lovejoy said, "A number of children were killed."[11]

These accusations are false and contradict accounts by other survivors who say women and children were not harmed. Local Mrs. Gordon Grosvenor wrote, "They (guerrillas) killed 180 men, but Charlie Hart (Quantrill) didn't molest women or children."[12] Local James C. Horton agreed, "If there was a woman or child harmed by Quantrill in Lawrence, I never heard of it."[13] Mrs. Elizabeth Earl, whose husband was a captain in the 9th Kansas Cavalry, added, "The women were not insulted as has been represented."[14] C. M. Chase wrote, "Bushwhackers have not yet raised a hand against a woman."[15]

---

7   Letter from George E. Young to My Dear Father, Aug. 23, 1863, Topeka, KS, Kansas State Historical Society.

8   Letter from Samuel R. Ayres to Lyman Langdon, Aug. 24-27, 1863, KSHS, Topeka, KS.

9   William E. Unrau (ed), "In Pursuit of Quantrill: An Enlisted Man's Response," *Kansas Collections: Kansas Historical Quarterly,* Autumn 1972, Vol. 39, No. 3, p. 384.

10   Greene, p. 435.

11   Julia Louisa Lovejoy, "Selected Letters from Kansas, 1855-1863," *Kansas Historical Quarterly*, Vol. 16.

12   *Kansas City Times*, July 5, 1961.

13   Gregg Manuscript.

14   Letter from Elizabeth S. C. Earl to Dear Brother, Sept. 22, 1863, Topeka, KS, Kansas State Historical Society.

15   C.M. Chase, Lela Barnes (ed), "An Editor Looks at Early-Day Kansas: The Letters of Charles Monroe Chase in Lela Barnes, (ed.), *Kansas Historical Quarterly*, Vol. XXVI, Summer 1960, p. 124.

After the war, a reporter asked William Gregg if the guerrillas killed women and children at Lawrence. He replied, "We waged no war on women and children," and added, "I also say that the honor of no woman was violated at Lawrence, and I enumerate instances where many guerrillas interposed and saved lives...I have tried to state just the facts."[16] However, two guerrillas said mistakes may have been made and owned up to it. Gregg wrote, "If any women and children were ever hurt by Quantrill's men it was an accident."[17] Andy Walker added, "Orders were to kill every man but to spare the women and boys; and while some women possibly were killed, I believe that any such instance was the result of accident, and not of murderous intent."[18] Gregg admitted the guerrillas mistakenly killed 14-year-old Bobby Martin because he was wearing his father's Union uniform and was misidentified as a soldier.[19]

Compassion for women: Saving homes and possessions

Concerning the women in Lawrence, historical evidence suggests in many cases, the guerrillas showed restraint, compassion, and sympathy. Survivor H. S. Clarke said guerrillas told him, "We do not want to injure widows, as Union men did with us."[20] Clarke added that during the raid, "Women were not harmed or insulted."[21] Former Kansas Governor Charles Robinson wrote, "Quantrill was more fortunate than Lane had been, as he told his prisoners taken at the Eldridge House, that he would spare the women from outrage, which Lane in his raids in Missouri did not do."[22]

---

16   *Ibid.*

17   Gregg Manuscript.

18   Eakin, p. 61.

19 In 1886, Mrs. Sarah E. Lanton wrote Marshall Prentice of Lawrence claiming she had been shot by a guerrilla and wanted the government to compensate her for her wound. Lanton's statement was printed in the *Lawrence Evening Tribune*, May 10, 1886.

20   Sheridan, H. S. Clarke, "The Remarkable Experience of One Family," p. 300.

21   *Ibid.*

22   Charles Robinson, *The Kansas Conflict,* (Honolulu, HI: University Press of the Pacific, 2004, reprint) p. 447.

*GURDON GROSVENOR – ITINERANT ABOLITIONIST MINISTER AND
FORMER CONNECTICUT MILITIA CAPTAIN WHO DRILLED LAWRENCE MILITIA.
(FROM HISTORY OF LAWRENCE, KANSAS BY CORDLEY)*

Many Lawrence women demonstrated a special charm with the guerrillas and succeeded in obtaining favors. One of these incidents occurred at the home of Gordon Grosvenor. As raiders approached the house, Mrs. Grosvenor told her husband, a hated itinerant anti-slavery preacher and military instructor for the local militia, to hide in a well adjacent to their home. The guerrillas stopped and asked if there were any guns in her house. She replied yes and surrendered four rifles to them. When the guerrillas failed to find her husband, they set fire to the home. Mrs. Grosvenor stopped the next group of guerrillas that rode by. One raider "removed his hat, bowed and said, 'William Quantrill at your service, Mrs. Grosvenor...Is your husband home?'"[23] Not

---

23 *Kansas City Times,* July 5, 1961.

wishing to lie, Mrs. Grosvenor replied that her husband was not in the house — which was technically accurate. She asked Quantrill if he might spare her home. Quantrill considered her request and ordered his men to put out the fire. After the war, a reporter interviewed Mrs. Grosvenor about her incident with Quantrill and thought it odd that, "In the several times we heard the story she showed a sneaking admiration for Quantrill."[24]

Another woman persuaded Bill Anderson to spare her home. According to the story, when Anderson informed her that the house was to be burned, she replied that her house and garden were too pretty to be burned. Anderson looked about the premises and backed down, saying, "Yes, by God, it is too pretty to burn and it shan't be burnt, by God, it shan't."[25]

There is a similar version of this story. This account states that as Quantrill was preparing to set fire to the home of George Ford, his wife met Quantrill at the door, and the two engaged in a conversation. She had a beautiful flower garden, and while the two were conversing, she plucked a flower and gave it to Quantrill. He then decided not to burn her house, and an eyewitness later saw Quantrill riding with her flower stuck in his hat.

But Quantrill wasn't the only raider to spare homes from destruction. When a guerrilla informed Miss Sophia Bissell that her home was to be burned, she pleaded, "Won't you spare the house?" Bissell recalled the man, "took off his hat and made a flourishing bow and said, 'For your sake, I will spare it.' "[26]

Guerrilla George Todd also saved homes. Todd stopped to talk with Mrs. E. P. Leonard (her husband was a Kansas officer), a native from England who had a broad British accent. He became intrigued with her and, before leaving, wrote 'Southern Confederacy' on the side of her house to save it from being burned. Todd then rode over to the Bullene House and made it his headquarters. While there, Todd was struck by the beauty of Mrs. Bullene's relative, Aunt Julia. Todd

---

24 *Ibid.*

25 Sheridan, Bailey, "Recollections of the Raid," p. 195.

26 Miss Sophia Bissell, "See Those Men! They Have No Flag." *American Heritage*, October 1960, Vol. 11, Issue 6.

Capt. William T. "Bloody Bill" Anderson – Missouri guerrilla. Killed at least 14 Lawrence men. (Wikimedia Commons)

CAPT. GEORGE TODD – MISSOURI GUERRILLA
HE SAVED LOCAL MEN'S LIVES AND FLIRTED WITH WOMEN. (FIND A GRAVE)

not only flirted with her but picked up her infant daughter, tossed her in the air, and kissed her. Before leaving, Todd handed a note to Mrs. Bullene instructing guerrillas not to burn her home.[27]

William Gregg also saved the home of Mr. and Mrs. Fred Read from being burned despite Read being a local militia member. Mrs. Read saw Gregg riding by and cried out, "You seem to be an officer, look at this house and at that burning store (their dry goods store on Massachusetts Street was on fire) and say if you have not punished us enough." Gregg pitied her and told his men, "Go away from here and tell all the other squads not to molest these premises any more today, this family has been punished enough."[28] To ensure its safety, Gregg stood guard over the home until the command withdrew from the town.

---

27 *Lawrence—Today and Yesterday*, "Commemorating the Semi-Centennial Memorial of the Lawrence Massacre, 1913, p. 124.

28 Sheridan, William L. Bullene, "The Appalling Scenes He Observed by William L. Bullene," p. 285.

MARY LANE – WIFE OF KANSAS SENATOR AND
GENERAL JAMES H. LANE. (LIBRARY OF CONGRESS)

Quantrill also demonstrated compassion for the wife of his bitter enemy, Jim Lane. When Quantrill informed Mary Lane that her house was to be burned, he left a group of men to help her remove furniture. An eyewitness testified, "There was a nice piano in the parlor and she was anxious to save it, so she asked some of the men to help her carry it out. They took hold of it readily and carried it to the door and finding that it was too wide to go through the door they left it. They however assisted Mrs. Lane and her two daughters in bringing up a lot of preserves and canned fruit from the cellar and pantry."[29] A similar incident occurred at the Sargent house. When told that their house was to be burned, the occupants were relieved to find the guerrillas quite courteous and helped them remove a piano from the home.[30]

---

29 Sheridan, Bailey. "Recollections of the Raid," pp. 44-45.

30 Lowman, pp. 91, 92.

The hated Reverend Hugh Fisher, chaplain, 5th Kansas Cavalry who participated in the burning of Osceola, Missouri, was home on leave at the time of the raid. When guerrillas came to his house, he hid in the basement and eluded his attackers. When Mrs. Fisher was told that the house was to be set on fire, one guerrilla offered to help her save her valuables. He said, "Madam, if there is anything you wish to save, I'll help you save it."[31] She asked if he would put out the fire, but the guerrilla replied he couldn't as it would cost him his life. Mrs. Fisher asked if they would delay setting the fire until she could remove the furniture. The guerrillas agreed, and a witness said, "The men waited for her to complete the work and even helped her with the heavy piano."[32]

Mrs. Peter Ridenhour was grief-stricken when guerrilla Jim Nolen said her house was to be burned. Nolen, however, gave her time to remove her valuables. After the guerrillas left, she was pleasantly surprised to find the guerrillas had "found a book full of family pictures which had been carried quite a distance from the house and laid on the ground near a tree." This prompted her husband, Peter, to write, "I have given them credit for a little kindness."[33]

---

31 Leslie, p. 227.

32 Griffith, p. 155.

33 Sheridan, Peter D. Ridenhour, "Hiding in a Potato Patch Saved His Life," p. 272.

CHAPTER 11

THE KILLINGS

POPULAR VERSION:

"The killing was indiscriminate and mostly in cold blood."

– Richard Cordley, Raid Survivor

CONFLICTING STATEMENT:

"They (guerrillas) knew just who they were after and where they lived."

– Sarah Fitch, Raid Survivor

INDISCRIMINATE VS. DISCRIMINATE KILLINGS

The Oxford dictionary defines massacre as "an indiscriminate and brutal slaughter of people." Survivor Richard Cordley believed the Lawrence Raid met the standard of this definition and wrote, "At Lawrence it was butchery from the first charge to the last shot...The killing was indiscriminate and mostly in cold blood...They killed whom they met without knowing who they were or caring what they were. ... The carnage was all the worse for the fact that the people were not expecting an indiscriminate slaughter."[1] Another survivor agreed with Cordley's assessment,

---

1   Cordley, *A History of Lawrence, Kansas*, p. 198.

saying, "Quantrill's invasion was a massacre and not a raid. It was not an attempt of armed men to disrupt the actions of other armed men but murder of innocent men."[2]

However, there is evidence that suggests the killings were discriminate, not indiscriminate. One survivor explained, "[The] guerrillas were killing methodically, not spasmodically. Each squad carried a list of specific persons slated to be killed and specific buildings marked for the torch."[3] Sarah Fitch added, "[The guerrillas] knew just who they were after and where they lived. They had marked their victims — and especially the members of the 'Independent Company' [local militia], of which Edward [her husband] was one of the first members — they had a list of that company."[4]

Judge Lawrence Bailey's recollection was like Mrs. Fitch's: "They had a carefully prepared list of the men to be killed. ... This list comprised the names of the best known abolitionists."[5] Samuel Reynolds added, "[The guerrillas] were evidently well acquainted with Lawrence, as the places and persons of active and prominent Union men were made the special marks of vengeance."[6] Another survivor noted, "The raiders had prepared lists of men they wanted dead and maps purportedly drawn by two women from Westport, showing the homes of the wanted men."[7] Another recalled the guerrillas "carried lists of the names of men they wished to kill in Lawrence, and there was a list made by the officers. In some instances the lists carried by individuals were copied from the general list. Many citizens heard these lists read off and consulted when the guerrillas were inquiring for certain parties."[8]

---

2   Betty Laird, Compilation of Articles, Letters, and Other Materials, Watkins Museum Archives, Lawrence, KS, August 21, 1929.

3   *Lawrence Journal-World*, Aug. 23, 1962.

4   Sheridan, Sarah Fitch, "A Letter from a Grief Stricken Young Widow," p. 260.

5   Bailey, p. 34.

6   Sheridan, "Editor's Commentary," p. 318.

7   *Kansas City Star*, Aug. 18, 1963.

8   Sheridan, "Editor's Commentary," pp. 317-318.

Survivor H. D. Fisher agreed the killings were not indiscriminate and said, "They (guerrillas) had a carefully prepared list of the men to be killed, a copy of which was picked up by a son of Mr. Stillman Andrews. ... This list comprised the names of the best-known abolitionists."[9] Another survivor remembered, "Many of the raiders had lists of names which they would consult after asking the name of a resident. They sought for well-known and prominent political and military persons with great pertinence. When they found them, they shot them down without mercy."[10]

REFERRING TO DEATH LISTS

An incident between local William Speer and an unidentified guerrilla provides an example of guerrillas referring to death lists. Speer was stopped by the raider, who asked for his name. William didn't want the man to know that he was the son of John Speer, a radical Danite, Jayhawker, friend of Jim Lane, and publisher of abolitionist newspaper the *Lawrence Journal.* He replied that his last name was Smith, not Speer. William recalled, "[The guerrilla] then took a long list of names, and I thought, looked them over, and then told me to hold his horses."[11] This incident demonstrates that if the guerrillas were killing indiscriminately, William would have been shot. However, because William Smith's name was not on the list, he was spared.

Survivor Robert G. Elliott offered his assessment of the killings: "A review of the situation made it apparent that indiscriminate killing, only so far as to prevent resistance, except in the case of soldiers, 'Red Legs,' and certain proscribed individuals, was an incident rather than a purpose."[12]

---

9   Bailey, p. 24.

10 Sheridan, "Editor's Commentary," p. 317.

11 Sheridan, William Speer, "My Story of the Quantrill Massacre," p. 304.

12 Elliott, p. 186.

TRADITIONAL EXAMPLES OF RAID VICTIMS

Researchers of the raid may notice that previously published books repeatedly rehash the killings of the same "innocent" victims. The official 'Lawrence Victims' list identifies slain soldiers from the 14th Kansas Cavalry and men they claim were innocent civilians. But the list fails to identify or ignores individuals who had past military experience or were members of the local militia. The following is a more complete description of the victims who always seem to be mentioned.

JUDGE LOUIS CARPENTER

Louis Carpenter was the judge of Probate Court for Douglas County, Kansas. A native of New York, Carpenter was a highly respected citizen. One local described him as being in delicate health and consequently unable to join the army. However, Carpenter was a staunch abolitionist, making him a candidate for the death list. Guerrillas visited Carpenter's house several times, but no one harmed him. As the guerrillas were preparing to leave, one final squad came by and shot him. The wounded Carpenter ran throughout the house and out into his yard attempting to escape. After he collapsed from blood loss, Carpenter's wife tried to shield his body from his attackers, but a guerrilla lifted her arm and shot Carpenter in the head.

One source however claims that Carpenter had been a colonel in the army and resigned his commission due to ill health.[13] If true, his military affiliation would automatically put him on Quantrill's death list.

CAPTAIN GEORGE W. BELL

G. W. Bell was the county clerk for Douglas County, Kansas. His house was located on Mount Oread. Hearing gunfire, he grabbed his cartridge box and musket to defend the town. His family begged

---

13   Leslie, p. 218.

CAPT. GEORGE W. BELL – 12TH KANSAS REGIMENT.
WRONGLY REPRESENTED AS CIVILIAN. (FIND A GRAVE)

him not to go, but Bell replied, "They may kill me, but they cannot kill the principles I fight for. If they take Lawrence they must do it over my dead body."[14]

As Bell headed downtown, he quickly realized that resistance was futile and hid among joists in an unfinished brick house. One guerrilla, supposedly an acquaintance, spotted him and convinced him to surrender. As Bell was being escorted downtown, another squad of guerrillas came by and executed him, first giving him time to pray.

A less dramatic account came from an eyewitness who recalled that when Bell saw the guerrillas, he jumped a fence and ran into a stable, where he was killed. This version does not mention Bell

---

14 Cordley, A History of Lawrence, Kansas, p. 201.

surrendering or praying.[15] Yet a third witness, Elise Englesmann Willemson, said Bell was on horseback, and the guerrillas surrounded and killed him. Erroneously listed as a civilian, Captain Bell was an officer in the 12th Kansas Regiment.

LEVI GATES

Levi Gates was said to have grabbed his musket and headed toward downtown when he heard shots. On his way, he saw two mounted guerrillas and fired at one. Gates apparently hit the raider as he was seen slumped in his saddle. The wounded man's comrade rode over and shot Gates. The guerrilla then dismounted and smashed Gates' head in with the butt of his rifle. Listed as a civilian non-combatant, Gates was a member of the local militia.

EDWARD FITCH

Edward Fitch was a popular schoolteacher. The guerrillas called Fitch to his door and shot him numerous times. They set fire to his house and watched as Fitch's body was consumed in flames. Survivor John Speer said Fitch was innocent writing, "[Fitch] never spoke of politics in school, [and] was wantonly murdered in his home, and the house set on fire."[16] What's missing from Speer's report is that Fitch was a Boston abolitionist, a member of the Free State Stubbs Rifles during Bleeding Kansas days, and a member of the local militia.

WILLIAM AND JOHN LAURIE

Listed as civilians, William and John Laurie were both Free State Stubbs Rifles members during Bleeding Kansas days. William was captured by the guerrillas during Quantrill's raid on Shawneetown, Kansas, but he escaped and moved closer to Lawrence. The two brothers rode into town on the night of Aug. 20.

---

15 Peter D. Ridenhour, *Quantrill's Raid: August 21, 1863: An Eyewitness Account,* (Lawrence, KS: Douglas County Historical Society, reprint), p.2.

16 Connelley, Quantrill and the Border Wars, p. 393.

The guerrillas captured both men during the raid. John, a member of the 14th Kansas Cavalry, begged for his brother to be spared, but a guerrilla replied, "We are not so particular about you, but that fellow (William), we will put him through."[17]

GRISWOLD, THORPE, BAKER, AND TRASK

One of the most misrepresented killings occurred with Griswold, Thorpe, Baker, and Trask. One source said that guerrillas came to their house and ordered them to surrender. Most sources state the men had one small pistol in their possession, and they consented to give up with the understanding they would be treated like prisoners and taken to the Eldridge House. The guerrillas agreed to their demands, and as they were heading toward the hotel, the deceptive guards shot them down in cold blood.

In contrast, another witness claimed the men were heavily armed and were radical pro-Lane advocates. Cordley wrote, "As the four men were well armed and were young and vigorous, they were disposed to remain in the house and defend themselves."[18] He said the guerrillas offered the men protection if they surrendered, and as they were taking them to the Eldridge House, another squad of guerrillas rode over and, without alerting their captors, shot them down.[19]

MEN SPARED AND PERMITTED TO ESCAPE

What's also missing from the historical record is the number of men the guerrillas spared. For example, after he escaped from camp, Pvt. Cosma Colman found shelter at the Rawlins home and was joined there by three other men. When the guerrillas came to the house, they told the occupants that they would not be harmed if they surrendered. The men complied, and the guerrillas left them unchanged. Colman insisted the guerrillas could have killed

---

17 *Ibid.*, p. 349.

18 Cordley, Pioneer Days in Kansas, p. 204.

19 Elliott, p. 188.

them and many other victims if they had wanted. Colman wrote, "Not one person was shot at or killed on our street after the first rush... At least a dozen could have been shot down had the patrol desired."[20] After the guerrilla command left, a drunken squad came by and killed two men who had been with Colman: G. H. Sergeant and W. T. Williamson.[21]

Guerrilla Capt. Dick Nolen is said to have spared a local from death. Nolen captured Col. James Blood, a militia member, as he was fleeing toward Mount Oread. The guerrilla robbed the Colonel and set him free. When Nolen discovered one of Blood's jewelry pieces had a picture of his son inside, he rode over and returned it to him.

Sgt. James E. Watson, also referred to as a civilian, was the quartermaster for the 2nd Kansas Cavalry. As he was escaping with his family, he was detected by two guerrillas who, ironically, had just deserted his company. His former comrades waved to Watson and permitted he and his family to find shelter. The guerrillas were overheard saying, "There goes our old quartermaster, and a good 'un."[22] The two guerrillas stood guard over Watson's house and prevented it from being burned. Sadly, after the command left town, Larkin Skaggs set it on fire.

In another example, David Brown, an elderly member of the local militia, surrendered his rifle to the guerrillas and walked among them without being molested.[23] Erastus Ladd had a similar experience as guerrillas observed him, but he was not harmed. He lived on Kentucky Street and, upon hearing gunshots, gathered his family to look for shelter. Ladd said of his experience, "When we had gone a few rods, one of [the guerrillas] crossed before us a few feet on another street, but he was walking his horse leisurely along. He glanced at us, but said nothing, and I made no effort to attract his attention, I assure. When we had gone about a mile, as we turned the corner of a fence, we saw two of their pickets some

20   Sheridan, Colman. "The Massacre of the Union Cavalry Recruits," p. 203.

21   *Ibid.*, p. 200.

22   Shea, p. 11.

23   Lowman, p. 90.

rods ahead of us. We turned to go in the opposite direction and confronted two more that way. As we approached them they turned and rode off towards some others, and left the road clear."[24]

O. A. McAllaster, a sergeant in the Kansas State Militia, was also permitted to escape. He lived on Rhode Island Street and followed three other locals, a Mr. Wood and Mr. and Mrs. Soule, seeking shelter. McAllaster said they were stopped by guerrillas, robbed, and permitted to seek safety in a cornfield. Local W. K. Cone was stopped by guerrillas but made his way safely to the Whitney House. Cone wrote, "Yet I escaped safely, and after being halted a few times by mounted pickets … who said as I was crippled they did not want me."[25]

Confederate Col. John Holt saved the life and home of H. S. Clarke, a Captain and an assistant provost marshal. As the two men talked outside his home, a guerrilla rode up and pointed his revolver at Clarke. Holt ordered him to put his gun down, saying that Clarke was his prisoner. When Holt was ordered to leave town, he warned Clarke, "Young man, I am going to leave you now. You will be killed as soon as I am gone if you stay where you are. My men are getting ready to leave. There will come others later, who are drunk and killing everybody they see. Go and hide. Go into the cellar." Turning to women nearby, Holt said, "Ladies, get that man (Clarke) out of sight if you want him to live. If parties come and inquire for him tell them that he has gone. If they start to burn your house, tell them that Colonel John D. Holt made this his headquarters and promised protection of property."[26]

George Todd saved the lives of Mat Shaw, Mr. House, and Mr. Prager. Todd had earlier permitted the men to remain with their families but insisted they get inside their home and stay away from windows and doors. Mat Shaw recalled what happened next: "He (Todd) was not gone more than two minutes, when another [guerrilla] came and ordered Mrs. Prager to tell us to come outside.

---

24   Erastus Ladd, "Erastus Ladd's Description of the Lawrence Massacre," Edited by Russell E. Bidlack, *Kansas Historical Quarterly,* 29, No. 2, pp. 113-121.

25   Cone, Roenigk, p. 11.

26   Sheridan, H. S. Clarke, "The Remarkable Experience of One Family," pp. 299-300.

With great presence of mind, Mrs. Prager screamed as loud as she could for the captain to return, which he did, and ordered the men away, and we both, Mr. Prager and I escaped death."[27]

In another example of sparing men, James Donnelley was captured and interrogated by guerrillas. Although Donnelly said he had nothing to do with the military, a few raiders wanted to kill him anyway. However, one guerrilla interceded and refused to let them molest Donnelley. As the squad was leaving, Donnelley thanked the guerrilla and asked his name. His rescuer declined, saying his sister lived in Lawrence, and he did not want her to get in any trouble.

Membership in the Masonic Order saved the lives of men in Lawrence. Masons are the oldest secret Fraternal Organization in the world dating back to the Middle Ages. To be eligible for membership, an individual must believe in a Higher Power. The purpose of the Masons is to uphold moral standards. These beliefs prevented guerrilla Masons from killing other members. The first instance occurred at the Eldridge House when Mason, R. S. Stevens, recognized Quantrill as a fellow member and succeeded in saving the lives of Masons Maj. Edwin P. Bancroft and Gen. C. W. Babcock. In addition, survivor H. B. Leonard told Connelley that when guerrillas surrounded local W. T. Williamson, he gave the group the Masonic sign of distress. Recognizing his sign, members in the squad persuaded the others to ride off and leave Williamson alone. Sadly, after Quantrill left, drunken guerrillas killed Williamson. Guerrilla John Jarrette was also a Mason and was known to have saved at least five Lawrence men who identified themselves as members.[28]

Popular versions of the raid wrongly depict a scenario in which victims were randomly selected and killed without rhyme or reason. They portray bloodthirsty guerrillas as killing anyone they came across. Yet, some raid survivors found it important enough to report that this was not the case. They describe the guerrillas following a more systematic and selective method in identifying victims.

---

27 *Lawrence--Today and Yesterday,* A Commemorative Magazine. 1913.

28 Houts, p. 68.

CHAPTER 12

VICTIM ANALYSIS

POPULAR VERSION:

"The men the raiders did kill were quiet peaceable citizens."

— Richard Cordley, Raid Survivor

CONFLICTING STATEMENT:

"There wasn't a citizen in the whole state of Kansas —— they were all soldiers."

— William Gregg, Guerrilla

Conflicting accounts exist about who the guerrillas were targeting during the raid. While guerrillas maintain their victims were military personnel, others suggest some of the killings were motivated by ethnicity and race.

ETHNIC AND RACE KILLINGS?

Historical reports suggest that Germans and Blacks were also singled out during the raid. One survivor commented, "Any negro or white man of German appearance who chanced to show himself was killed instantly." He concluded, "The same treatment was accorded the residential section, where the search was on for men known to have participated in Jayhawking outrages in Missouri."[1]

---

1   Dwight D. Stinson, "The Bloodiest Atrocity of the Civil War," *Civil War Times, Illustrated,* December, 1963, p. 45.

BLACK CASUALTIES

Reports do not agree about the number of Blacks killed, but research suggests it was very few. Many believe this was because they were employed as domestic servants and already awake when the guerrillas attacked. Upon hearing shots, they quickly found shelter. Another source added that on August 20, the evening before the raid, Blacks saw strangers, later known to be guerrilla spies, lurking about town, and made contingency plans to escape. The Blacks who were killed were old men caught out in the street. These men included Uncle Frank, Uncle Henry, Benjamin Stonestreet, Mr. Ellis, and Anthony Oldham.[2]

However, testimony suggests that a more significant number of Blacks were killed than initially believed. Some accounts say that as many as 50 to 60 were victims. Sources explain that this omission is because many families never returned to Lawrence and resulted in many Black victims never being identified.

GERMAN CASUALTIES

As far back as the 1840s, pro-Southern Missourians developed contempt for Germans who immigrated in mass from their homeland to Missouri. As a hard-working, industrious group opposed to slavery, when the war erupted, the majority joined the Union army. Pro-Southern Missourians believed Germans who joined the Union Army were no better than hired foreign mercenaries akin to the German Hessians during the Revolutionary War. They gave them the derogatory moniker 'Lopped-Eared Dutch.' As the war progressed, German families living in western Missouri moved to Kansas, where their political views were consistent with the majority.

Before the war, the German men in Lawrence formed a social club called the *Turnverein*, an organization that focused on physical fitness and the study of military tactics. In 1861, 48 local Germans belonged to this club, and when the war erupted, 44 joined the Union

---

2   It was common for older Black men to be called 'Uncle.'

army.[3] Germans worshiped at the Church of the Brethren, whose minister, S. S. Snyder, was a Lieutenant in the 2nd Kansas Colored.

Most Germans lived on the 800 block of Massachusetts Street, where their stores (an incredible number of 20 whiskey saloons) were located.[4] During the raid, a witness recalled, "Here chaos reigned."[5] Survivors say the guerrillas showed the Germans no mercy. Guerrilla Kit Dalton recalled, "Massachusetts Street, where the riff-raff of the old world, downeasters and niggers were encamped...Scavengers from the slums of Ireland, Germany, Norway and Sweden, nihilists from Russia, and anarchists from Poland, and runaway niggers from every portion of the south were there...They all perished in the streets...All male adults found in the city were destroyed and that without mercy."[6]

Demonstrating his hatred towards Germans, one guerrilla saw August Ehlis (Ellis) take his infant son in his arms and hide in an adjacent cornfield. When his son began to cry, the guerrilla found Ehlis' hiding place. He shot Ehlis and left his son in his dead father's arms. Joseph Brechtlesbauer, a saloon owner on Massachusetts Street, was bedridden in his upstairs home. His family carried him outside, where a guerrilla shot him. After the raid, the Rev. Frederick L. Pilla (the clergyman from Eudora) visited Lawrence and claimed that at least 30 Germans were killed on Massachusetts Street.[7] These victims included Mr. Swan, George Oehrle, August Ehlis, Louis Wise, Jacob Pollock, James Brechtlesbauer, John Zimmerman, George and Samuel Range, George Gerard (Gerrard), and Henry Albach (by mistake).

---

3   Sheridan, "Editor's Commentary," p. 337.

4   Edward and Sarah Fitch, Postmarked: Bleeding Kansas, Letters from the Birthplace of the Civil War, Pioneer Dispatches from Edward and Sarah Fitch (Topeka, Kan.: Purple Duck Press, 2013), p. 239.

5   Sheridan, "Editor's Commentary," p. 338.

6   Captain Kit Dalton, Under the Black Flag: Guerilla Captain of the Confederacy, Border Outlaw with Frank and Jesse James and Texas Ranger (Memphis, Tenn.: Larry J. Tolbert, Originally published in 1914, Reprint in 1995), p. 23.

7   Sheridan, "Editor's Commentary," p. 338.

MILITARY PERSONNEL KILLED

Yet, the guerrillas maintained that most of their victims were affiliated with military organizations, whether they were militia members, Jayhawkers, or Red Legs. The *Lawrence World Journal* denied this suggestion, writing, "Quantrill ... knew that this city was not a military station and that no troops were here to defend it."[8] Conflicting with this statement, another survivor admitted, "There were a large number of military men in town."[9]

Guerrilla T. C. Miller declared, "Many Federal soldiers were slain. They begged to be taken prisoners, but Quantrill reminded them of (Union) General Halleck's orders (Extermination Policy issued March 13, 1862) and of the hundreds of old men they had killed in Missouri."[10]

After the war, Gregg was asked if guerrillas killed innocent citizens. He replied, "They said we killed citizens in Lawrence... That's not so. There wasn't a citizen in the whole state of Kansas... They were all soldiers — every man big enough to carry a gun was a soldier — and we killed them in retaliation for the killing by the Redlegs."[11] Gregg continued: "At the time of the Lawrence Raid, the entire male populace of Kansas was soldiers, minute men, organized and equipped by the government. I tell these facts to show the world that Quantrill and his men only killed soldiers in Kansas... May a just God wreak vengeance on the guilty."[12] A reporter asked another guerrilla veteran the same question, and he responded that the men in Lawrence were "thieves, murderers, or outlaws...If you lined up the citizens of Lawrence and fired into them for a half hour with a Gatling gun...you would not have killed an honest man."[13]

---

8   *Lawrence Daily Journal,* Sept. 8, 1891.

9   Cordley, A History of Lawrence, Kansas, p. 198.

10   *The Liberty Tribune,* Liberty, Missouri, April 1, 1910.

11   William H. Gregg, "The Lawrence Raid," typescript. 5 pages, Topeka, Kansas, Kansas State Historical Society.

12   *Ibid.*

13   *Kansas City Times,* Dec. 8, 1975.

QUANTRILL LEAVES LAWRENCE

At 9 a.m., lookouts on Mount Oread notified Quantrill that the Union cavalry was approaching Lawrence from the east. Survivors heard a high-pitched whistle coming from South Park, signaling the guerrillas to assemble. It's important to remember at this juncture that Quantrill's men were composed from an assortment of independent commands who banded together for the sole purpose of attacking Lawrence. In other words, not all the guerrillas recognized Quantrill as their leader and as has been seen, some threatened to kill him. Aware that there were rogue guerrillas he had no control over, Quantrill warned his Whitney House prisoners to stay inside because these men would be looking to kill more victims. With that, "[Quantrill] politely raised his hat to the ladies and hoping that their next meeting might be under pleasanter conditions, bade them good day and rode off." [14]

As the guerrillas gathered in South Park, Quantrill ordered Gregg to stay behind to round up stragglers. He told Gregg he would wait one hour for him just south of Blanton's Bridge.

GUERRILLAS WHO KILLED THE MOST AND "THE LOOSE GANG"

Based on the popular version of the raid, it would be easy to think that all the guerrillas were involved in the killing; but evidence suggests otherwise. In fact, Connelley initially believed Quantrill designated 12 men to be his official death squad freeing others to burn and loot. [15]

While this number is low, testimony shows as few as 25, and no more than 50 guerrillas did all the killing. H. S. Clarke wrote, "of the 300 men in the raider's gang, probably not over 50 did the murderous acts, but we blamed them all alike." [16] William Miller

---

14 Sheridan, Winchell, "The Sacking of Lawrence," p. 180.

15 Joseph M. Beilein, Jr., (ed), *William Gregg's War: The Battle to Shape the History of Guerrilla Warfare,* (Athens, GA: University of Georgia Press, 2019), p. 101.

16 Sheridan, "Editor's Commentary," p. 315.

agreed, saying, "The shooting was done by only a few men, three quarters of the men probably never fired a shot."[17] H. S. Clarke added, "I am of the opinion that all the killing was done by less than fifty men."[18]

So, who were the 50 or so men that did the killing? While there is no conclusive answer, one group of guerrillas that survivors called the 'Loose Gang' were probably the culprits. The author believes this company was led by Bill Anderson and composed of men from Jackson and Cass Counties. The following is the author's interpretation of the Loose Gang's actions.

After the Eldridge House surrendered, the Loose Gang rode over to west Lawrence to Gen. Collamore's house and set it on fire. Afterward, the men saw Griswold, Thorpe, Baker, and Trask being escorted to the Eldridge House. The Loose Gang rode over and, without warning to the original captors, who had promised them protection, shot them down. They also saw Capt. George Bell surrendering to a guerrilla who had also promised Bell's protection and killed him. Returning to Massachusetts Street, the Loose Gang tried to kill Quantrill's Eldridge House prisoners as they were escorted to the Whitney House. After Quantrill's command left town, 12 drunken members of the Loose Gang stayed behind and looked for more victims.

The first person they murdered was Daniel W. Palmer, who owned a gun shop located next to the 14th Kansas Cavalry's camp. The guerrillas spotted Daniel and his son Charles inside their store. They shot and wounded both men and set their store on fire. The guerrillas then tied father and son together and threw them into the store, burning them alive.

Another victim was Sylvester Dulinski, who, ironically, was Quantrill's friend. The guerrilla chief had previously told his men not to harm him. Dulinski lived south of town on the Fort Scott Road and, when informed that the guerrillas were attacking Lawrence,

---

17   Connelley Collection, William Miller Reminiscences.

18   H. S. Clarke, "Incidents of Quantrill's Raid on Lawrence," *Kansas Collections: Kansas State Historical Society,* Vol. 7, 1901-1902, p. 10.

replied they were his friends. Dulinski is thought to have previously boarded Quantrill and allowed his spies to stay at his home.

Dulinski met his fate after Quantrill's central command passed his house. A few minutes later, 12 drunken members of the Loose Gang rode by Dulinski's house. He waved to them and yelled, "Hurrah for Jeff Davis." One of the guerrillas took offense at Dulinski's gesture, thinking he was making fun of the group. A witness wrote, "Dulinski was killed by the last squad of guerrillas that left Lawrence...[He] was killed by some guerrilla who was either drunk and irresponsible or who did not know his relations with Quantrill's band...One of them presented a pistol at him and ordered him to come out to the fence. He replied that he would if the guerrilla would lower his pistol. The guerrilla fired and killed Dulinski."[19]

Many ask who the individual guerrillas were who killed the most victims? Testimony suggests that Bill Anderson (14 victims), Larkin Skaggs (13 victims), and Peyton Long (at least 14 victims) killed the most men. In an interesting twist, evidence suggests George Todd, who many believed was on a murderous rampage, was too busy flirting with women to be involved in the affair. It is also worth noting that Dick Yeager's company had their hands full robbing stores on Massachusetts Street to participate in the killings.

Blood Lust: The Rev. Larkin Skaggs, Guerrilla

The author believes that Baptist minister Larkin Skaggs was a member of the Loose Gang. Skaggs killed John M. Speer, son of abolitionist and Jim Lane's friend, John Speer, and attempted to steal Lydia Stone's ring before being forced to return it. After Quantrill's command left, a drunken Skaggs, with three other guerrillas, rode over to the Whitney House with the intent of killing Lydia and her father. Prisoner Robert Stevens recalled Lydia running past him and hiding upstairs from Skaggs. Skaggs called for the prisoners to come out, saying, "Here, you God damn sons of bitches, come out here... Come out here, all of you!"[20] While some complied, others stayed

---

19 Sheridan, William Brown ,"The Killing of Citizens in South Lawrence," p. 245.

20 Bailey, p. 15.

inside. Skaggs shot and wounded three men before Quantrill's friend, Nathan Stone, interrupted the proceeding.

Stone scolded Skaggs and told him that Quantrill had promised protection for his occupants. Skaggs responded by shooting Stone in the abdomen, a wound he died from hours later. Skaggs then saw militiaman and judge Sam Riggs come out of hiding and rode after him. Riggs' wife, Kate, seeing that Skaggs was about to shoot her husband, grabbed his horse's bridle and pulled it so hard that he could not accurately fire his pistol, saving her husband's life. Consequently, Skaggs rode off, looking for easier victims. He went over to Fred Read's house, although William Gregg had just spent 30 minutes protecting it from being burned, and attempted to it on fire, but every time he lit a match, Mrs. Read blew it out.

Frustrated, Skaggs saw George Burt in the street and demanded his money. After Burt emptied his pockets, Skaggs shot and killed him. Skaggs then saw Dennis Murphy standing in his front yard and ordered him to fetch a cup of water. Murphy complied, and as Skaggs reached for the water with his left hand, he shot Murphy with his right.

Skaggs finally realized he was alone and out of ammunition. Thinking the guerrillas had gone east, he rode out on the road to Eudora. But Skaggs had waited too long, and a local posse captured him. This posse has been the center of discussion as some question their identity. Described as farmers, the men included Miles Walters, Thomas McFarland, John McFarland, Robert Peebles, and others. However, military records show John McFarland enlisted as a private in the 13th Regiment Kansas Volunteers and deserted in 1862, making him a suspected Red Leg. So, were the other men with McFarland Red Legs too?

As this posse was returning to town with Skaggs, another group of 25 to 30 unidentified mounted men (Red Legs?) caught up and halted them. What happened next has never been agreed upon, as one source recalled, "We have received five or six accounts of [Skaggs] being killed in five or six different places, by five or six different parties."[21]

---

21 Betty Laird, *A Compilation of Articles, Letters, and Other Materials,* Newspaper Clipping, Sept. 15, 1915, Douglas County Historical Society, Lawrence, Kan.

WHITE TURKEY – KILLED SKAGGS.
(FROM HISTORY OF LAWRENCE, KANSAS *BY CORDLEY)*

One version states a 'volunteer' rode over to Skaggs and struck him in the face with his fist. He told Skaggs, "Get off that horse and go." As Skaggs ran for his life, another man galloped after him, firing his pistol, but his shots missed. One bullet, however, grazed Skaggs and set his shirt on fire. White Turkey, a Delaware Indian, shot Skaggs with an arrow, the shaft traveling through his body and protruding out his ribs. Skaggs continued to run until another Indian, Little Beaver, shot him through the heart with his buffalo rifle.[22]

Skaggs' body was tied to a horse and dragged through Lawrence until his corpse was mutilated. He was hung from a tree, where locals fired bullets into his body. Skaggs was eventually cut down and dragged to a ravine, where his body was set on fire and left to rot.

---

22 *The Lawrence Journal-World*, Sept. 15, 1915.

White locals blamed Negroes for mutilating Skaggs' body. Reporter C. M. Chase initiated this account, saying he saw "a *negro* rushing through the streets on horseback, dragging the dead body of a dead rebel, with a rope around his neck hitched to his saddle. A crowd was following pelting the rebel with stones."[23]

But others suggest whites were simply using blacks as a scapegoat. One black witness, Andrew Williams, said the individuals who killed Skaggs (the posse) were the culprits. Williams wrote that they had "taken [Skaggs] and hitched a rope around his neck and attached a horse and drug him all over town and then taken him down to a ravine and put him in it and burned him up."[24] Pvt. Cosma Colman also witnessed the killing of Skaggs and made no mention of Negroes having anything to do with Skaggs' body. Colman wrote, "Some of our men put a lariat around one of his legs and hitching the other end to the pommel of the saddle, dragged him up to the corner of Massachusetts and Henry Street on a gallop."[25]

The popular version of the raid portrays the entire guerrilla command as randomly dispatching every person they came across. The evidence, however, demonstrates that a small number of men were involved in the killings. Many of the most brutal executions were committed by a band of 12 drunk guerrillas who murdered with impunity after Quantrill left Lawrence. Last, testimony demonstrates that victims were not aimlessly chosen but had been previously selected and documented on paper by Quantrill and his officers.

---

23 Connelley, *Quantrill and the Border Wars*, p. 382n.

24 William A. Dobak, ed., "Civil War on the Kansas-Missouri Border: The Narrative of Former Slave Andrew Williams," *Kansas History*, Vol. 6, No. 4, Winter 1983-84, p. 240.

25 Sheridan, Colman, "The Massacre of the Union Cavalry Recruits, pp. 200, 201.

Chapter 13

THE PURSUIT

POPULAR VERSION:

"Lane ordered Rankin to attack Quantrill and took his place at the head of the column...Lane got far in advance where he rode towards the enemy alone."

– William Connelley, Kansas Historian

CONFLICTING STATEMENT:

"When the last we heard of [Lane], he was riding along head down, in the rear of our forces, urging them."

– Albert Greene, 9th Kansas Cavalry

After the guerrillas left Lawrence, Delaware Indians and soldiers from the 12th Kansas Infantry crossed the river into town. They arrived with a certain amount of fear and trepidation as one admitted, "Quantrill and his 300 devils were leaving just as we entered the place. We should be pleased to announce that the occasion of our entry is what frightened the demons out of Lawrence, but as these letters are devoted to truth-telling, we are compelled to admit that the scare was on the other side and had not Quantrill been evacuating at the east of town, we should have been hastily engaged in an undertaking of that nature at the west end. It

*LT. COL WILLIAM A. RANKIN – COUSIN OF COL. JOHN K RANKIN.
SURVIVED RAID. (FROM* HISTORY OF LAWRENCE, KANSAS *BY CORDLEY)*

is a proud thing for one to relate his courageous deeds, but on this occasion it would be improper for us to enlarge upon that subject."[1] With the guerrillas gone, Union officers Capt. F. B. Swift, Capt. Andrew Shannon, Lt. Col. John Rankin, Capt. William Rankin, Col. James Blood, Gen. George Dietzler, Gen. C. W. Babcock, Lt. George Ellis, Capt. J. A. Abbot, Maj. Ansom Storm, Capt. John Wilder and other soldiers came out of hiding.

SEN. JIM LANE ORGANIZES THE PURSUIT

At the beginning of the raid, Lane and his servant ran to a ravine two miles away. Four hours later, his servant returned to town, saw Robert Morrow, former commander of Lane's Northern Army,

---

1   Charles Monroe Chase, "An Editor Looks at Early-Day Kansas, The Letters of Charles Monroe Chase," edited by Lela Barnes, Kansas *Historical Quarterly*, No. 26, Autumn 1960, p. 292.

and led him back to Lane. Morrow said he found Lane "completely bewildered, did not know where he was...and [asked] if he had better get further off."[2] Later, John Stillman Brown saw Lane returning to town and wrote facetiously, "To my surprise I found coming up from our ravine the brave Gen. James H. Lane our United States Senator, and soldier. I told him the way was all clear."[3]

Indeed, one source said it took Lane one hour and 30 minutes to find clothes, a horse, and ride into Lawrence to organize a posse. Having recruited 30 men armed with an assortment of weapons, Lane's recruits rode after the raiders. While testimonies report Lane courageously led his troops against the guerrillas, others were not so complimentary. One soldier recalled, "When the last we heard of him [Lane] was riding along head down, in the rear of our forces, urging them."[4]

Quantrill's Retreat From Kansas

Quantrill's command rode south on the Fort Scott Road and crossed Blanton's Bridge, where they waited for Gregg to gather the stragglers. Quantrill sent a squad farther west to McGee's Crossing to burn two houses belonging to Dr. Eliab Macy, a conductor for the Underground Railroad.

Another group of guerrillas also visited the home of Abraham Rothrock, who lived 10 miles south of Lawrence. Rothrock was a German Dunkard minister, and his son, Hi, was a member of the 9th Kansas Cavalry. Hi joined the pursuit and rode with Col. George Hoyt, making him a Red Leg suspect. While the guerrillas were eating, Abraham entered, and the raiders asked who he was. When he identified himself as a minister, they replied they had orders to kill all preachers and shot him. Although wounded, Rothrock survived.

---

2   *The Daily Times*, Leavenworth, Kan., Sept. 4, 1863.

3   Letter from John Stillman Brown to John L. Rupur, Sept. 1, 1863, Topeka, KS, Kansas State Historical Society.

4   *Ibid.*

An interesting event took place while the guerrillas were waiting for Gregg. Mounted next to Quantrill, Frank James looked back into town and saw 60 men ride into Lawrence. James believed they were Red Legs and gave this information to his chieftain. James asked if they should go back and attack them. Quantrill said no because he could see Union cavalry coming in from the east. Could these be the same men who captured Skaggs and thought to be Red Legs?

After Gregg rejoined the command, the guerrillas continued south and arrived at Brooklyn, where they found the town abandoned. Earlier in the day, locals saw smoke coming from Lawrence and hid in adjacent cornfields. Brooklyn consisted of a general store, saloon, livery stable, inn, and five or six homes. The guerrillas burned all the buildings except the store and saloon. As they were firing the town, the commands of Jim Lane and Col. Preston Plumb united north of the village.

How The Kansans' Pursuit Developed

Back on the evening of August 20, when Ewing's spies reported at his Kansas City headquarters, they were told the general was AWOL. Ewing, thinking nothing of consequence would occur for a few days, left his post without permission from General John Schofield. Ewing told his adjutant, Colonel Preston Plumb, he was going to Fort Leavenworth to visit his ailing wife. But some sources say he took a French leave — a romantic visit. The general could only be contacted by telegraph, but on the night of August 20, the fort's telegraph officer was absent.

Alerted to the spies' information, Plumb mobilized the 11th Kansas Cavalry to pursue the guerrillas. Unfortunately, this unit was in the process of transitioning from infantry into a cavalry unit, and the men had no experience fighting on horseback. One source confirmed, "The men, unaccustomed to use their arms on horseback, had no confidence in themselves or each other."[5]

---

5   Bailey, p. 33.

Col. John Rankin, who had confronted the guerrillas in Lawrence, joined Lane's posse of thirty-five that pursued Quantrill. He recalled that Lane did not want to engage the raiders but wanted to ride to Baldwin City to pick up the militia stationed there. His plan was interrupted when told that Plumb's command was riding towards them.[6] The two commands united north of Brooklyn. With the guerrillas in sight, an argument between Lane and Plumb concerning who was in control brought the pursuit to a standstill. One soldier wrote, "Some precious minutes were wasted while [Lane and Plumb] argued over which of them should take command of the pursuit."[7] Lane finally permitted Plumb to lead.

A REAR GUARD ACTION

The guerrillas wanted to attack the Kansans when they spotted them outside Brooklyn, but Quantrill said it was a bad idea. He remarked, "No, we will not fight 'em. In the first place, we haven't enough ammunition to make a stand; in the second place, our horses are not able to make a charge."[8]

The guerrillas continued south with Union cavalry following. Skirmishes between the two forces broke out near the Jardon and Fletcher houses. During one of these charges, guerrilla Fletcher Taylor broke from the Kansan's ranks and rejoined Quantrill's command. Taylor had inadvertently been left behind in Lawrence and was luckily wearing a Union uniform. He convinced the Kansans he was a Union officer and joined the pursuit. Taylor broke away during one of the skirmishes and entered the guerrilla ranks; fortunately, being recognized before being shot. Months later, Quantrill and Taylor reflected on this incident. As the story goes, "Quantrill asked Taylor what he would have done if a guerrilla who could have identified him had been captured and taken to him. Fletch said he would have executed the guerrilla. Quantrill said Fletch was selfish, to sacrifice the life of another to save his

---

6   Connelley Collection, Statement of John K. Rankin.

7   Stinson, p. 45.

8   Eakin, p. 64.

FLETCHER TAYLOR – MISSOURI GUERRILLA OFFICER
(WILSON'S CREEK NATIONAL BATTLEFIELD)

own. Quantrill replied that he would have identified Fletch so they both would have been executed together."[9] Taylor was offended by Quantrill's response and soon left the command. After the war, Taylor became a harsh critic of Quantrill.

Having passed the Fletcher farm, the guerrillas rode toward a ford that crossed Ottawa Creek. Capt. Coleman anticipated the guerrillas' movement and sent Plumb's soldiers down the east side of the creek to block this movement. Coleman informed Plumb he was going charge the guerrillas' rear in hopes the two forces would

---

9   Connelley Collection, Letter from W. L. Potter to W. W. Scott, Feb. 29, 1869, Topeka, KS, Kansas State Historical Society.

surround and annihilate them. While Plumb rode off on his flanking maneuver, Coleman charged through a cornfield. One witness described his attack: "When [Coleman's men] came to the fence on the other side of the field, they saw Quantrill's men drawn up in line, a little distance in advance, at the mouth of a lane." A Kansas officer shouted, "Throw the fence and charge." Another screamed, "Dismount boys, and give them a round or two with your Burnsides at three hundred yards."[10] The soldiers fired one volley into the ranks of the guerrillas before being dispersed.

When Quantrill saw the Kansans charging, he turned and attacked. Guerrilla Frank Smith recalled Todd shouting, "Boys, let down those rail fences, part of you go up one side through the corn and part of you follow me right up to the lane and by God, we'll charge them. We've got to check them or the whole outfit is lost."[11] Quantrill's attack drove the Kansans back to their main command. While Coleman's men were regrouping, Plumb, who was supposed to have blocked the ford, returned. Coleman was furious with Plumb, and choice words were exchanged between the two officers. So, why did Plumb fail to carry out his mission? There are three possible explanations. The first was that his horses were worn out and could not reach the ford before Coleman attacked. The second was that Plumb rode to the sound of the guns, a standard cavalry policy. The third was that he was a coward.

The Kansans' volley killed four guerrillas, and their bodies were left where they fell. During the attack, a few guerrillas retreated to the head of the main column, causing confusion. After Quantrill regrouped his men, he said, "Now, if any of you intend to break ranks again, do it now; if you stay with me and act like men, I can get you out of this, but if you are going to run, go now, but do not come back to me."[12] With this warning, Quantrill ordered his officers to shoot any man who broke ranks.

---

10 Capt. Holland Wheeler, "Statement of Captain Holland Wheeler," Lawrence, KS, Spencer Research Library.

11 Castel, Notes from Frank Smith Manuscript.

12 Barton, p. 127.

Quantrill turned to Gregg and said, "Organize your sixty men into a skirmish line and hold the rear. Fall back on the main line whenever necessary. But whatever you do, do not let them break your line."[13] Gregg commanded the rear guard most of the day until he was forced to yield to Todd, having lost his voice from shouting commands.

Plumb had 1500 troops in his command, giving him a considerable advantage in numbers. But he continued to stay at a safe distance from the guerrillas. Lieutenant Cyrus Leland lost his patience and received permission from Plumb to cut 50 men out to skirmish with the guerrillas. Leland said of his efforts: "Whenever we would press up pretty close and commence firing on the enemy, they would halt and form in line of battle, and fight us until our cavalry would come in sight or come pretty near their range when [the guerrillas] would commence their retreat again. Our cavalry horses were very much worn out and could not catch up with the advance militia."[14]

While Leland was fighting, he recalled Plumb's command remained "one to five miles in our rear," posing no threat to the guerrillas.[15] Trooper Albert Greene, riding with Leland, remarked, "We skirmished all day with this rear guard, firing a few shots at long range, but as our main command seemed averse to giving us any support and kept out of sight most of the time, we let it go at that."[16] Like Leland, Greene was disappointed with Plumb's lack of aggressiveness and wrote, "Perhaps it would be more correct to designate [the pursuit] as escorting the bushwhackers out of Kansas and back to their homes in Missouri, for at no time were they pursued with any apparent purpose to overtake and punish

---

13 Gregg Manuscript.

14 Letter from Leland to Dear Mother, Sept. 2, 1863, Topeka, KS, Kansas State Historical Society.

15 *Ibid.*

16 Greene, p. 441.

CPL. ALBERT R. GREENE – 9TH KANSAS CAVALRY
(COLLECTIONS OF THE KANSAS STATE HISTORICAL SOCIETY)

them."[17] Another soldier added that Plumb "took the pursuit very leisurely and when the bushwhackers slowed up, Plumb would slow up too."[18]

The guerrillas' rear guard was effective in keeping the Kansans at bay. Their skillful performance prompted one pursuer to write, "Their rear guard was commanded by a daring fellow (Gregg or Todd) and their horsemanship of the dozen men who covered the retreat was superb. These men carried no plunder and their horses were guided entirely by the legs of the rider, leaving both hands free to use revolvers. When they finally turned to race after the command the riders bent far forward, almost to the necks of their horse, and seemed to be a part of them."[19]

---

17   *Ibid.*, p. 445.

18   Blair, p. 201.

19   Greene, p. 440.

Just south of Spring Hill, the two forces momentarily lost sight of each other. Greene was ordered to take a spyglass to the top of a hill and report his findings. When he reached the summit, Greene said he didn't need a spyglass, as "There below me and within a mile was Quantrill's whole command."[20] Seeing that Plumb's troops were coming up, Greene believed the time for revenge was near. He returned to his company and said his fellow soldiers (he reported 300 men) were "spoiling for a fight." To his disbelief, the order to attack never came.

To Greene's consternation, Colonel Edward Lynde called for a council of war. Greene was upset and remarked, "With the enemy in striking distance; with the way open and the road plain and unobstructed; with a force superior in numbers, arms and discipline and a majority of the men and horses fresh, just what urgent necessity existed...never can be explained." He said the troopers yelled, "Hit the trail – hit the trail. ... They'll be in the Grand River timber while we're fooling here."[21] After Lynde completed his officers' conference, he ordered his troops to unsaddle and graze their horses.

At this point, Greene recalled, "Pandemonium broke loose, and discipline, and even ordinary respect for a superior officer, were thrown to the winds. Captains Coleman and [Henry] Flesher called Lynde an arrant coward to his face and repeated it again and again and interlarded the charge with profane adjective." After an hour's rest, Lynde ordered his bugler to sound, "Forward," but Greene said they rode to the foot of a hill, and "The order was given, 'Prepare to dismount.'" Greene wrote: "Here was mutiny, pure and simple." The disgusted soldiers eventually complied.[22]

Toward the end of the day, the guerrillas were nearing Paola, Kansas. While on an elevation, Lieutenant Leland saw Kansas troops massing in town and believed he still might be able to trap Quantrill in a pincer-like movement. Leland attacked the guerrillas' rear guard in hopes of forcing them toward Paola. He succeeded in

---

20 *Ibid.*, pp. 437-438.

21 Greene, p. 437.

22 *Ibid.*, pp. 437, 438.

driving them over a rise and onto their main column. Quantrill was also aware that Kansas troops were in Paola and took steps to avoid being surrounded. He called his men together and said, "I'm going to charge 'em again (Leland's troops), and I want every man that's got a horse able to gallop to come with me."[23] The guerrillas charged over the brow of the hill and straight into Leland's command. Leland described the attack: "We had just driven the rear guard of the enemy over the brow of a hill when we heard yelling just over this hill. Soon we saw the enemy come up on the hill. They were in line, I think, about 200 strong. They came charging down upon us. We fell back to this company of cavalry."[24] With darkness coming on, Leland reorganized his men and rode into Paola, having temporarily lost Quantrill's trail.

The guerrillas took advantage of Leland's retreat by bypassing Paola to the north and crossing a ford at Bull Creek. They rested for an hour until Kansas scouts discovered them. Quantrill then ordered his weary guerrillas to remount, and they continued toward the state line. As dawn approached, Quantrill saw 1,200 Union Missouri troops waiting for him at the border and knew he had 1,500 Kansans in his rear.

When the guerrillas crossed into Missouri, they were met by the 4th Missouri State Militia under the command of Lt. Col. Austin King. Quantrill was not in favor of engaging these troops and said, "Now every man who thinks his horse is able, follow me to Big Creek; those not able, take care of yourselves in the timber of Grand River."[25] Andy Blunt's company rode to Cass County while Quantrill, Todd, Yeager, and Holt continued to the Sni and Blue rivers in Jackson County.

The Kansans pursued the guerrillas so closely that three wounded guerrillas, who had been placed in an ambulance, were abandoned and hidden among the brush, their comrades promising to return

---

23 Eakin, p. 68.

24 Robert S. Laforte, "Cyrus Leland Jr. and the Lawrence Massacre: A Note and Document," *Kansas History: A Journal of the Central Plains,* Vol. 9, No. 4, Winter 1986/87, p. 179.

25 Eakin, p. 68.

the next day. The wounded men were Ab Hallar, William Bledsoe, and Tom Hamilton. It wasn't long before Indian scouts found the men and signaled the Kansans to join them. Hallar and Hamilton begged for their lives, but Bledsoe said, "Stop it! We are not entitled to mercy! We spare none and do not expect to be spared." Bledsoe asked the soldiers to take them out of the ambulance and put them on their knees facing them before being executed.[26] The guerrillas were hauled out of the wagon and shot. The Indian scouts were permitted to scalp the guerrillas and cut off their ears.[27] At this time, Samuel Boyce (Boise) came out of the timber and joined the Kansans. The guerrillas had taken Boyce prisoner at Lawrence and forced him to drive the ambulance that carried the wounded raiders.

The next day, Andy Blunt's company returned to retrieve their wounded comrades but found them dead and their bodies mutilated. Blunt commented, "We have something to learn yet, boys, and we have learned it. Scalp for scalp hereafter."[28]

GUERRILLA RAID CASUALTIES

A total of seven guerrillas were killed during the retreat from Lawrence. One man was captured south of Spring Hill and executed by a firing squad. A Kansas trooper said of the guerrilla: "[He] was a young man of good appearance and address, with a cool, quiet manner that marked him as one who had faced death too often to feel fear of its approach."[29] He continued, "The shots took effect in his breast, and for a moment before falling, he stood erect coolly looking around to see if more shots were to be fired. His bones now lie in an unmarked grave where he fell."[30]

Another guerrilla was killed when he was discovered drunk in the middle of the road, holding on to a rope fastened around a calf's head. As the Kansans approached, the raider stopped and bowed

---

26   Connelley, *Quantrill and the Border Wars,* pp. 415-416.

27   Banasik, p. 33n.

28   Houts, p. 72.

29   Blair, p. 201.

30   *Ibid.*

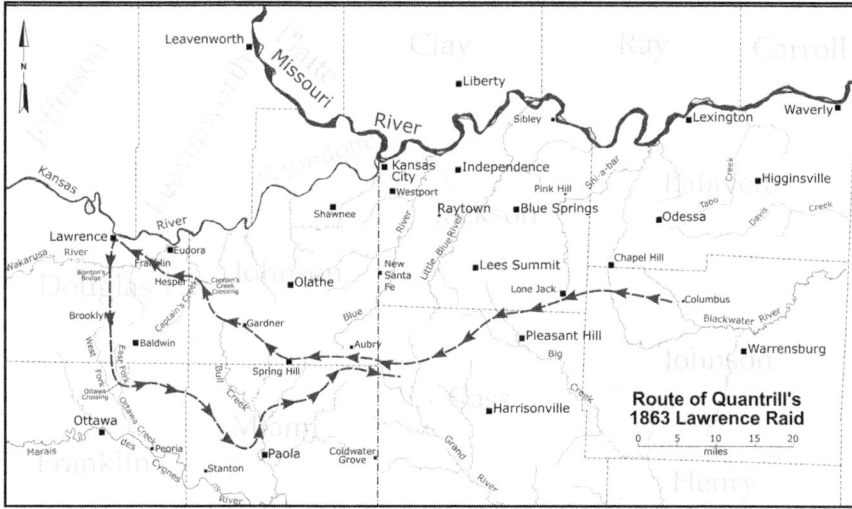

QUANTRILL'S ROUTE FROM BLACKWATER RIVER TO LAWRENCE
AND RETURN TO MISSOURI – (CIVILWARMUSE)

to his pursuers. He was shot on the spot.[31] Three more guerrillas were captured and executed by their pursuers. Red Leg Col. George Hoyt told a prisoner, "I will just kill you for being a damned fool." Another Red Leg, Theodore Bartles, shot the other two raiders.[32]

RED LEGS PRESENT DURING PURSUIT

Trooper Albert Greene, a suspected Red Leg, confirmed that Red Legs Col. Hoyt and Theodore Bartles were with him in the advance party with Leland. The presence of these men suggests that perhaps more Red Legs participated in the pursuit. [33] If this is true, the question is, at what point did they join Plumb's troops? Connelley said the Red Legs joined on August 22, but historian Alice Nichols believed the Red Legs linked up in Lawrence and followed the guerrillas back to Missouri. Nichol's statement corresponds with Frank James' claim that he saw Red Legs entering Lawrence after the guerrillas left. Other prospective Red Leg members

---

31   Greene, pp. 439-440.

32   Connelley, *Quantrill and the Border Wars*, p. 413.

33   Greene, p. 439.

who participated in the advance company with Hoyt and Bartles included Jeff Denton, Andy Hammond, Bud Myers, Bob Huston, John Moore, Ed Kinney, Hi Rothrock, a member of the 9th Kansas Cavalry, Albert Greene, 9th Kansas Cavalry, and Graydon McCune.[34]

JAYHAWKERS AND RED LEGS PURSUE GUERRILLAS IN MISSOURI

The most significant number of guerrilla casualties occurred after Quantrill disbanded his command. Many were forced to abandon their tired horses and find safety in the brush. Lt. Leland captured and hanged one alleged bushwhacker at his home and executed another in front of his wife. Near Lone Jack, he found three more suspected guerrillas and hanged them so high in a tree that riders could pass beneath them without being able to touch their feet. Leland put up a sign that read, "Don't Cut Them Down."

General Ewing finally caught up with the pursuit on the night of August 21 and wrote Gen. John Schofield, "No prisoners have been taken and none will be."[35] Ewing reported his troops had already killed 100 Missourians. Guerrilla William Gregg said of the guerrilla losses, "In the six days after we got back to Missouri from the Lawrence raid we lost more men than we lost on that famous expedition."[36]

The evidence demonstrates that Col. Plumb's command was afraid of the guerrillas and made no heroic attempts to stop their progress back to Missouri. Quantrill remained cool during the retreat and was successful in getting his troops out of several potentially disastrous situations.

---

34 *Ibid.*, p. 439.

35 Charles Mink, "General Orders, No. 11, The Forced Evacuation of Civilians during the Civil War," *Military Affairs,* Vol. 34, No. 4, Dec. 1970, p. 133.

36 Gregg Manuscript.

Chapter 14

ORDER NUMBER ELEVEN

POPULAR VERSION:

"[Order No. 11] was an act of wisdom, courage, and humanity, by which the lives of hundreds of innocent people were saved... Not a life was sacrificed, nor any great discomfort inflicted in carrying out the order. The necessities of all the poor people were provided for and none was permitted to suffer."

— Union Major General Henry W. Halleck

'

CONFLICTING STATEMENT:

"The number of those killed [during Order No. 11] was never reported, as they were scattered all over western Missouri."

— The Reverend George Miller, Missourian

ORDER NO. 11

On Aug. 22, Senator Lane and Gen. Ewing, commander of the District of the Border, met at a cabin outside Morristown, Missouri. Lane threatened to have Ewing dismissed from service if he didn't agree to take drastic measures against the guerrilla supporters in western Missouri. Ewing didn't have a choice as he was embarrassed about being AWOL when Quantrill attacked.

Consequently, he drafted Order No. 11, which mandated residents from the Missouri counties of Jackson, Cass, Bates, and parts of Vernon be banished within 15 days. Although Ewing commanded troops from Illinois, Colorado, Missouri, and Iowa, he designated his revenge-seeking 15th Kansas Cavalry and Red Legs to enforce the order. Ewing also reactivated the commission of the notorious Col. Charles Jennison and ordered him, with Red Leg Col. George Hoyt, to clean out the area. It was the recipe for a disaster that ended with hundreds of Missourians being murdered.[1]

In Richmond, Virginia, the Daily Dispatch was outraged with the brutality that Order No. 11 brought: "Quantrill's raid upon Lawrence, Kansas, seems to have provoked a war of extermination against the people of Northern Missouri."[2] Historian Albert Castel described Order No. 11 as "the most drastic and repressive military measure directed against civilians by the Union Army during the Civil War."[3]

Guerrilla Andy Walker recalled, "Southern men were shot at their thresholds in the act of obeying the order, and their effects seized by their greedy murderers. In every direction, dense columns of ascending smoke marked the destruction of our people's homes. Long trains of wagons heaped with our household goods and supplies were to be seen moving Kansasward."[4]

Missouri minister George Miller wrote, "Unarmed old men and boys were accused [of being guerrillas] and shot down, and homes with their now meagre [sic] comforts were burned, and helpless women and children turned out with no provision for the approaching winter."[5] *The New York Times* said, "Not a day passes

---

1   For more information regarding Order Number Eleven, see Tom A. Rafiner, *Cinders and Silence.*

2   Mink, "General Orders, No. 11: The Forced Evacuation of Civilians During the Civil War," *Military Affairs,* Vol. 34, No. 4. (Dec. 1970), p. 132.

3   Albert Castel, "Order Number 11 and the Civil War on the Border," *Missouri Historical Review,* July 1963, p. 57.

4   Eakin, p. 72.

5   George Miller D. D., Missouri's Memorable Decade, 1860-1870: A Historical Sketch, Personal, Political, Religious (Columbia, Mo.: Press of E. W. Stephens, 1898), pp. 100-101.

that does not chronicle house-burning and murders."[6] Missourian, Mrs. J. M. Thatcher, said her husband was incarcerated without a trial and executed two weeks later. Mrs. C. C. Rainwater recollected, "[Men were] called to the door at night and shot down without warning or provocations."[7] Historian Nichols said Red Legs "slew every man that they came to, without inquiring into his politics."[8] One Jayhawker bragged that he had single-handedly killed 30 suspected guerrillas in Lafayette County, Missouri.

Not all Union officers supported Ewing's decision to allow Kansans to enforce Order Number Eleven. Union Maj. and Missourian Austin King believed the victims they killed were defenseless, saying, "Truthful and loyal Union men of that county all knew that only unarmed civilians had been killed."[9] One newspaper said, "We have found ourselves asking: Can it be possible, that this is the work of an officer wearing the uniform of our country?"[10] Missourian Wiley Britton, a member of the 6th Kansas Cavalry, was upset about the way Kansans were treating his native people. Britton argued, "Our people (Kansas troops) should remember that Missouri has sent to the field, including her state troops, nearly one hundred thousand union men; upwards of six times the number furnished by Kansas. Are the loyal people of Missouri entitled to no sympathy? If the reports be true, and I have endeavored to get at the exact truth, the Missouri state troops have followed Quantrill more persistently, and killed more of his men, than have our Kansas troops, that were stationed along the border."[11]

The exact number of Missourians killed during Order No. 11 has never been calculated, but it certainly meets and likely exceeds

---

6   *The New York Times*, Sept. 22, 1863.

7   Matthew Christopher Hulbert, Ghosts of Guerrilla Memory: How Civil War Bushwhackers Became Gunslingers in the American West, (Athens, Ga.: University of Georgia Press, 2016), p. 122.

8   Alice Nichols, *Bleeding Kansas*, (New York, NY: Oxford University Press, 1954), p. 258

9   Michael Fellman, Inside War: The Guerrilla Conflict in Missouri During the American Civil War (New York: Oxford University Press, 1989), p. 43.

10   Mink, p. 133.

11   Miller, George, p. 103.

the 180 victims in Lawrence. George Miller mentioned it was impossible to account for the number of Missouri deaths, writing, "The number of those killed was never reported, as they were scattered all over western Missouri."[12] Sources say Missouri men simply vanished after they were arrested and were never heard from again. This occurrence was confirmed by a Missourian who survived his incarceration. The prisoner testified, "Men were taken out of the prison at a late hour almost every night and never heard of again."[13] George Miller added, "Many [Missouri prisoners] were put out of the way so secretly, that their relatives, never knew how or where, but only, that they never came home again. Human bones and unknowable graves were found in out-of-the way places, for two or three years after the war closed; sometimes a bleached skeleton still dangled from a tree in some dark timbered dell — God only knowing the doers of the deed."[14]

Former Kansas Gov. Charles Robinson regretted the number of Missouri victims who suffered during Order No. 11 and wrote, "The victims of his (Quantrill's) massacre have been counted, but those whom Lane and Jennison left in the hands of their executioners, who will chronicle them? They are unnumbered as the murders of Attila [the Hun]."[15]

To cover up the brutality and bloodshed of Order No. 11, Union Gen. John Schofield sent a letter to Ewing praising him for issuing the order and emphasizing its humanitarian effort toward Missourians. He wrote, "[Order No. 11] was an act of wisdom, courage, and humanity, by which the lives of hundreds of innocent people were saved...Not a life was sacrificed, nor any great discomfort inflicted in carrying out the order. The necessities of all the poor people were provided for and none was permitted to suffer."[16]

---

12 *Ibid.*, pp. 100-101.

13 *Ibid.*, p. 101.

14 *Ibid.*, pp. 100-101.

15 Charles Robinson, *The Kansas Conflict*, (Reprint, Honolulu, HI: University Press of the Pacific, 2004), p. 461.

16 W.L. Webb, *Battles and Biographies of Missourians: or the Civil War Period of Our State* (Kansas City, MO: Oak Hills Publishing, 1900), p. 254.

Chapter 15

SPIES AND CONSPIRACIES

POPULAR VERSION:

"Kansas should be laid waste at once. This was the one idea of Quantrill. It was ever present in his mind. The one object of his life was to enter Kansas with an adequate force, and then burn and murder."

— William Connelley, Kansas Historian

CONFLICTING STATEMENT:

"I Believe Genl. Lane and His Element were in collusion through third persons with Quantrel [sic]."

— Charles Robinson, Former Kansas Governor

QUANTRILL SPIES

Substantial evidence exists that points toward several Lawrence residents colluding with Quantrill and aiding him in planning his attack. The following individuals are suspects:

SYLVESTER DULINSKI lived south of Lawrence on Fort Scott Road. Sources say he harbored pro-Southern spies. On the day of the raid, when told that Quantrill's men were attacking Lawrence, Dulinski replied that the guerrillas were his friends and would not harm him. A drunken guerrilla killed Dulinski against Quantrill's orders.

MATTIE LYKINS was from Kentucky and moved to Missouri in 1842. She was known for her outspoken support for the South. Mattie had two brothers: one a Missouri guerrilla, the other a Confederate spy. Her stepson, W. H. R. Lykins, lived in Lawrence and was a pro-Southern supporter. Mattie was suspected of meeting with Quantrill in Kansas City before the raid and providing a map of Lawrence that pointed out the residences of radical abolitionists and military leaders. Mattie was in Lawrence the day of the attack and stayed at the home of her stepson, W. H. R. Lykins. Their lives and property were not threatened. Mattie was afterwards accused of being a spy, and some authorities wanted her hanged, but they instead agreed to banish her from western Missouri. She later married artist George Caleb Bingham, an outspoken critic of Kansas Jayhawkers.

W. H. R. LYKINS was Mattie Lykins' stepson. He was an early settler in Lawrence and, during the "Bleeding Kansas" period, was known to support the pro-Southern Missourians. Lykins was part owner of a bank located across the street from the Eldridge House and was one of Sallie Young's individuals she supposedly "saved." His home was not damaged, and he was taken as a prisoner to the Whitney House. Lykins' guilty conscience may have caused him to have a mental breakdown as years later he was reported as being in a deranged state of mind and attempted suicide.

JAMES CHRISTIAN was a pro-slavery man from Missouri. He worked as an attorney in a law office with Jim Lane. During the struggle for statehood, Christian supported the pro-slavery government. At the time of the raid, Christian was a captain in the 12th Kansas Cavalry and was saved by Sallie Young. Like Lykins, he found safety inside the Whitney House.

JAKE CALLEW (aka Tom Curlew) was a Missourian who lived in Lawrence with his wife and children. On the night of Aug. 20, he moved his family out of town. During the raid, Callew was seen riding with guerrillas and pointing out the homes of the victims. He was captured and accused of being a spy. Callew was taken to a barn to be hanged. Locals threw a rope over a joist, and Callew stood on a dry-goods box while a noose was placed around his neck. The box was kicked away, and as his body thrashed about, several men filled him with bullets.

Witness H. B. Leonard gave another version of Callew's hanging. He said that local Jonathan Oldham presided over a mock trial and ordered Callew hanged. Leonard said the victim never spoke during the court proceeding but spent his time whittling away on a stick. He remembered that as soon as Callew was strung up, a man by the name of Pickens jumped on his back and tried to break his neck. His effort failed, and when Callew was let down, he convulsed on the ground. A man named Charley O'Connell stepped forward and shot Callew two or three times in the head.[1] Capt. Alexander Banks presented another account, saying, "The 'cuss' wasn't hung skillfully and wouldn't die, so I had to order my men to shoot him, at the word 6 rifle balls put him out of misery."[2] Some sources contend that four more men were tried as spies, but their fates are unknown. It's believed a father and son by the last name of Dally and two men with the last name of Wallace were tried by a kangaroo court.

SALLIE YOUNG was a native of Ireland and came to Lawrence from Lecompton, Kansas, the pro-Southern territorial capital. At the time of the raid, she stayed at the former pro-Southern Territorial Gov. Wilson Shannon home and was employed as a seamstress at the Eldridge House. On the morning of the attack, she had risen early to go on a horseback ride with John Donnelly, a private in the 12th Kansas Infantry, Steve Horton, and Nin Beck. The guerrillas spotted them and pursued the party. Young was the only one captured, and she was taken to Quantrill. She claimed the guerrillas forced her to point out the homes of individuals on the death list.

Young complied with the raiders' request and was seen riding and laughing with guerrillas. Her involvement prompted one witness to say, "On Aug. 20 all were sent away, and that night the raid came, revealing the spy in the person of an attractive young lady from Missouri, who had been in Lawrence several weeks

---

1 Connelley Collection, Statement of H. B. Leonard.

2 Letter from Alexander Banks to Brother, Sept. 9, 1863, Kansas State Historical Society, Topeka, KS.

mingling in society."[3] Another wrote, "A striking feature of the heartless scene was a lady in a riding habit, contrasting with the careless and dingy garb of her escort, accompanying a squad and seeming to lead them, riding with the abandon of the boldest raider, and scurrying from house to house, parleying at each in her circuit of dwellings in west Lawrence."[4] When Lawrence women saw Sallie riding with the guerrillas, they called her a "Dirty se-sech devil" and "Bitch from Hell."[5] Survivor Laura M. Anderson said she had been suspicious of Sallie because she "had seen her ride out with men in the early morning often that summer."[6]

Sallie Young was arrested and charged as a spy. Emotions ran high and some wanted her hanged but calmer minds sent her to Fort Leavenworth for interrogation. At her trial, Young claimed she had saved the lives of men by telling the guerrillas they were relatives or friends. When asked to name the individuals she saved, Sallie identified W. H. R. Lykins, James Christian, and Governor Shannon, all pro-Southern men. Young was found not guilty and released. She married and moved to Emporia, Kansas. She afterward refused to talk about the raid.

CONSPIRACY THEORIES

POLITICAL AND FINANCIAL GAIN FROM THE RAID

Professor Burton J. Williams believes that factors other than revenge led to Quantrill's raid. Williams wrote, "There is increasing evidence to support the suspicion that the success of the Quantrill raid was assured by 'insiders' who for personal, political, or economic reasons stood to gain from the selective destruction of Lawrence."[7] Let's explore this theory.

---

3   Cone, Roenigk, (ed), p. 7.

4   Elliott, p. 187.

5   Crafton, p. 203.

6   Connelley Collection, Statement of Laura M. Anderson.

7   Burton J. Williams, "Quantrill's Raid on Lawrence, Kansas: A Question of Complicity," *Kansas History, A Journal of the Central Plains,* Summer, 1968, Vol. 34,

DID COL. CHARLES JENNISON COLLUDE WITH QUANTRILL?

Some believe Quantrill, Jennison, and the Red Legs all conspired together. So, how would this arrangement work? The facts show that Jennison owned a freighting company in Leavenworth that had a contract with the United States Army to supply military forts out west. Because his business required livestock, it has been asserted that Quantrill stole Missouri livestock and delivered them to Jennison for cash. If true, this would make anti-jayhawker Governor Charles Robinson a threat to Jennison's business. Life would be easier for Jennison if Robinson and his followers were out of the way. One newspaper reinforced this theory, writing, "Quantrill's operations were connected directly through parties at Leavenworth City with the U. S. Government at Fort Leavenworth... That in fact Quantrill, the Red Legs, Jayhawkers, odd members of the M. S. M. (Missouri State Militia) together with a few citizens of Jackson County are all acting in concert for the purpose of a general system of plunder in this section of the country."[8]

This was not the first time that Quantrill and the Red Legs were thought to be cooperating with each other. One person said, "Quantrill was on friendly terms with the quasi-military bandits known as the 'Kansas Red Legs' whose base of operations was Lawrence." He continued saying that Quantrill's relations with Red Legs "were of the most friendly character — so much so that they never did each other any harm in battle or otherwise — and Quantrile's (sic) plunder of horses, mules, cattle and valuables has frequently been found in the market in Kansas."[9]

No. 2, pp. 143-149.

8   *Liberty Tribune*, December 26, 1862.

9   Letter from John G. Beeson to W. W. Scott, (No Date), Lawrence, KS, Spencer Research Library.

Did Charles Robinson Collude
With Quantrill?

Other conspiracy theorists suggest that former Governor Charles Robinson colluded with Quantrill to get his nemesis, Jim Lane, killed. Indeed, Robinson had many reasons to get rid of Lane.

Lane and Robinson had been at odds with each other since "Bleeding Kansas." Back then, Robinson wished to avoid violence with pro-Southerners while Lane promoted it. After Robinson became governor, Lane succeeded in having him impeached over his alleged mishandling of state bonds (an allegation that cost Robinson his governorship. He was later exonerated).

Lane continually usurped Robinson's authority as governor. President Abraham Lincoln gave his support to Lane rather than Robinson. At one point, Robinson even accused Lane of trying to assassinate him when he attempted to disband his Red Legs.

At the time of the raid, Lawrence was negotiating with the L. P. and W. Railroad company about land purchasing. Robinson and Lane both owned stock in the company and had land they hoped the railroad would buy. The successful seller would be rewarded with a financial windfall. Lane's property was south of Lawrence, while Robinson's was north. Both men were members of the railroad Board of Directors, but Lane succeeded in having Robinson dismissed. Thanks to Robinson's attorney, R. S. Stevens, who visited with Quantrill at the Eldridge House and also owned stock in the railroad, the railroad purchased Robinson's land.

Robinson's behavior on the day of the raid was, at the very least, suspicious. He awoke early and went to check his horses on Mount Oread just before Quantrill attacked. During the raid, Robinson was said to have sat down in the open and watched the attack. He did not attempt to help or interfere. Guerrilla sentries saw Robinson but did not attempt to disturb him. Connelley tried to explain this awkward scenario, writing, "Even in this terrible massacre during the Lawrence Raid and when the doctor slowly retired from his barn to the brow of Mt. Oread, near where several of Quantrill's men were on guard, they did not molest him. There was a certain

CHARLES ROBINSON – FIRST KANSAS GOVERNOR.
(FROM THE LIFE OF CHARLES ROBINSON BY BLACKMAR)

something, a strange commanding influence, a pressure that neutralized, for the time being, any power to do him wrong."[10]

But Missouri historian Martin Ismert dismissed Connelley's explanation and stated, "This is a very strong wording and infers that Robinson had an understanding with Quantrill. We all know that Robinson hated Jim Lane, mostly due to Lane's looting, burning and murdering in the Missouri border counties. Dr. Robinson never did tolerate Lane."[11] Indeed, raid survivors recall Quantrill telling them he wanted to spare Robinson because he had tried to rein in the radical abolitionists in town. Quantrill said of Robinson, "While governor, he did what he could to preserve peace on the border, [and] he should not molest him or his property."[12]

---

10   Ismert, p. 1.

11   *Ibid.*, p. 1.

12   Connelley, *Quantrill and the Border Wars*, p. 371.

Curiously, Connelley's research suggests he too may have believed Robinson colluded with Quantrill. While reviewing Connelley's papers at the Kansas State Historical Society, I noticed a note Connelley made to himself. On a notepad when he writes about Quantrill driving a buggy to the top of Mount Oread, Connelley scribbled in the margin, "[This] ... is evidence also that Quantrill went to Mount Oread to have a talk with Governor Robinson."[13]

DID JIM LANE COLLUDE WITH QUANTRILL?

Others believe Senator Jim Lane planned the raid with Quantrill. This belief is not as crazy as it sounds because as far back as 1856, Free State men from Kansas continually worried about Lane being on too friendly terms with pro-slavery men.

On the day of the raid, Lane found shelter in a cornfield behind his home and made no effort to confront the guerrillas. His action, or perhaps lack of it, led many to believe Lane was using Quantrill to kill his political enemies, especially Charles Robinson. One raid survivor believed Lane ordered the murders of Griswold, Trask, and Baker because they opposed him. This source wrote, "These men were not shot at random; they had been designated beforehand. Many believe that the persistent assertions of Josiah Trask's widow that her husband was killed by Lane had some foundation. On the other hand, what prominent friend of Lane was killed intentionally as such? Not one. Whose house in all the city, was protected by a guard — Lane's attorney, Gov. Shannon. ... Will it be said that Lane has no fellowship or communication with proslavery men?"[14] Survivor R. G. Elliott was another who believed Lane colluded with Quantrill and wrote that pro-slavery men "and the notorious Lane [were] lying down together ... growing fat in their purses and persons by speculation."[15]

Charles Robinson directly accused Lane of working with Quantrill and wrote, "I have no doubt that men in our state knew

---

13 Connelley Collection.

14 Council Grove Press, Sept. 14, 1863.

15 R. G. Elliott to Dear Sister, May 8, 1857, Topeka, KS, Kansas State Historical Society.

all about it (the attack on Lawrence) ...I believe Genl. Lane and his element were in collusion through third persons with Quantrel (sic). I have no proof of it and no one out of Kansas would believe such a thing possible and hence I am not disposed to say anything about it publicly. ... The world never will know nor believe the insanity, or deep depravity of some of our politicians, especially of one [James H. Lane]."[16]

The spy and conspiracy information are intriguing and begs for a more thorough investigation to determine the underlying genesis of the raid.

16   Charles Robinson to A. A. Lawrence, Lawrence, Oct. 6, 1863, "Robinson papers" manuscripts division of the Kansas State Historical Society.

Chapter 16

DETAILS OF THE RAID

POPULAR STATEMENT:

"No, the guerrillas had no sufficient cause for the Lawrence Massacre."

— William Connelley, Kansas Historian

CONFLICTING STATEMENT:

"This foul murder [of our women when the jail collapsed] was the direct cause for the famous raid on Lawrence, Kansas. We could stand no more...We were determined to have revenge."

— John McCorkle, Guerrilla

THE DAMAGE INFLICTED AT LAWRENCE

After the smoke cleared, Lawrence survivors began to take inventory of the damage the guerrillas had inflicted. They found that three banks had been robbed of $250,000 and 182 buildings destroyed. The Miller block, located just to the south of the Eldridge House, and the armory were the only two buildings left standing on Massachusetts Street. The Miller block was probably spared because Missouri Reverend George Miller was a friend of Quantrill and this section was owned by his brother, Josiah.

Raiders burned three hotels, 100 stores robbed, destroyed three printing presses, and burned 70 homes and one African American church. Total damages came to $2,250,000. Yet, guerrilla William Gregg disagreed with survivor accounts regarding the amount of personal property lost. He argued, "I have always contended that the fires we started that morning destroyed as much property that had belonged to Jackson County people as that belonging to the citizens of Lawrence."[1]

NUMBER OF LAWRENCE VICTIMS

The exact number of individuals killed during the raid has never been determined. The Reverend Cordley, who participated in the burials, said he could only account for 146 victims. Yet, over the years, this number has grown to 180. Regardless, this result is dramatic when put in perspective. At the time of the raid, Lawrence had an estimated population of 2,000 people. Of that number, 400 men were supposedly present on the day of the attack. Given that there were 180 victims, this means that the guerrillas killed nearly half the men in Lawrence.

NORTHERN ASSESSMENT OF RAID

With the aid of raid survivors, the Northern press excoriated the guerrillas for their attack and labeled it an unprovoked massacre of innocent victims. Their argument was based on the spurious premise that Lawrence was unprotected, and their inhabitants were peace-loving defenseless victims. Similar versions were fueled by survivors like judge Lawrence Bailey, who wrote, "[The Lawrence Raid was]... one of the most unprovoked and cold blooded massacres that occurred during the war, by which unarmed and defenseless men lost their lives."[2] One newspaper added, "With a band of close to 500 men, Quantrill, then a captain in the Confederacy, rode into Lawrence, destroyed businesses and homes, [and] butchered

---

1 *Kansas City Star,* Sept. 25, 1898.

2 Bailey, p. 50.

men, women, and children."[3] Another paper wrote, "According to accounts, 150 men, women, and children were slaughtered and raped by Quantrill's men."[4]

Survivor John Speer added to the false narrative asserting that Lawrence had done nothing to provoke an attack from the guerrillas. He denied that his friend, Jim Lane, and his Kansas troops had committed harm in Missouri. Speer remarked, "If there was a single town, or a hamlet or a farmhouse which [Lane] burned, or an individual whom he maltreated in his acts of war, I have never heard one of them named; and yet, the horrible massacre at Lawrence — the brutal murder in cold blood of 180 defenseless persons after the town was surrendered — have been justified as retaliatory measures for Lane's outrages in Missouri...There never was an individual case named where Lane murdered any man, before or after the Quantrill massacre."[5]

PRAISE FOR QUANTRILL'S USE OF MILITARY TACTICS

In terms of military strategy, many scholars praised Quantrill for his meticulous planning and execution of the raid. Dr. Castel wrote, "[Quantrill] deserves credit for the raid's success. He conceived it, planned it, and led it. From a purely military standpoint it was a brilliant feat. Especially worthy of admiration are the courage and determination he displayed in carrying it out, and the magnificent timing which enabled him to strike Lawrence just at dawn and to retreat back to Missouri before the enemy forces could concentrate against him."[6]

---

3   *The Advance*, Higginsville, Mo., Oct. 9, 1992.

4   *The Times Recorder*, Oct. 24, 1982.

5   John Speer, "The Burning of Osceola, MO, by Lane and the Quantrill Raid Contrasted," *Transactions of the Kansas State Historical Society,* Vol. 6, 1900, p. 308.

6   Castel, p. 143.

Writer Lloyd Lewis agreed: "Quantrill, if viewed objectively, was a great cavalry man, probably as skillful as General Nathan Bedford Forrest."[7]

DEFENDING QUANTRILL'S RAID ON LAWRENCE

There were others who did not censor Quantrill's attack on Lawrence. Alice Nichols wrote, "There is considerable evidence to support the contention that the bushwhacker's fiendish sack of Lawrence in 1863 added up to no more brutality than had been imposed on Missouri and Arkansas civilians by Jim Lane's unauthorized brigade and by that flying squadron known as the Kansas Redlegs, a brutal band that flaunted its identity by wearing morocco leggings."[8]

Missourian, B. J. George, whose father participated in the raid, added, "We do not object to an all-out war to win. We do not object to all-out war as used against our family in Jackson County. What we do object to is the hypocrisy of the North shedding crocodile tears over Lawrence while piously contriving to use [the same] methods already set up, and partially put into effect against the Southerners of Missouri — open all-out war under phony excuses. One can more easily explain and excuse stupidity than hypocrisy!"[9]

The *Oak Grove Banner* supported Quantrill's attack, writing, "We make no excuse for the Quantrill raid, for it was only a repetition of the Jayhawker, Red Leg style. But for every person killed in Lawrence, the Missouri counties can show 15 killed, for every house burned in Lawrence, 25 were burned...by Kansas desperadoes... Our Lawrence friends should remember when they get on the high

---

7   Lloyd Lewis, "Propaganda and the Kansas-Missouri War," *Missouri Historical Review*, No. 34, October 1939, p. 11.

8   Nichols, p. 255.

9   B. J. George, The Gregg Biography-Captain William Henry Gregg, Confederate Officer, Quantrillian Officer, and Good Citizen: Dabs about the author of Gregg... little dab of history without embellishment, (Columbia, MO: B. James George , 1973), p. 93.

moral plain that Lawrence was for years headquarters for the worst gang of thieves, cutthroats and murderers that ever gathered on any part of the green earth."[10]

Kansans' Allegations Against Guerrillas

After the attack, there were survivors who made damaging allegations against the guerrillas including accusations of cowardice and drunkenness. Let us review these issues.

The Issue Of Cowardice And Drunkenness

In his book, Connelley pointed to survivor John Wilder's experience as proof the guerrillas were cowards. Wilder lived in a stone house, and when guerrillas made no serious attempt to molest him, Connelley pronounced them cowards. However, Connelley fails to mention three essential facts about this event. First, houses made of stone won't burn; second, Wilder was a captain in the 3rd Kansas State Militia and armed with a shotgun; and third, 18 men were hiding in his house and believed to be armed.[11]

Missourian B. J. George responded to Connelley's assertion that the guerrillas were cowards. He wrote, "Connelley wrote that at no time in Lawrence did the guerrillas show bravery or daring. Could he say that the slinking, hiding citizens of Lawrence showed bravery or daring? Just how many brave acts were committed by citizens that day? Does not the list of dead guerrillas tell the story?"[12] Guerrilla William Gregg agreed, "At Lawrence, no Kansan seemed to have a burning desire to take as many Missourians with him as he could in death, and that in an era when very many persons had arms and ammunition, and usually knew how to use them, in defense of their homes at least."[13]

---

10 *Oak Grove Banner,* Sept. 22, 1905.

11 Connelley Collection.

12 George, B. J. p. 73.

13 *Ibid.*

Regarding the allegation of drunkenness, the facts show that a group of 12 guerrillas were intoxicated and brutally killed individuals after Quantrill left town. But as for the rest of the command, B. J. George argued, "If they (guerrillas) were drunk as some claim, they were the most competent drunks we have ever read about in war!"[14]

It would be impossible for anyone today to suggest that Quantrill's raid was justified. Censorship and threats of social rejection curb most individuals from making such statements. This makes the comments of these turn of the century Missouri apologists even more interesting.

---

14 *Ibid.*, p. 80.

CHAPTER 17

FINAL THOUGHTS

FINAL THOUGHTS

The most well-known guerrillas who participated in the Lawrence raid did not live long afterward. Bill Anderson and George Todd were both killed in 1864 while participating in Confederate Gen. Sterling Price's invasion of Missouri. In May 1865, Quantrill left Missouri with a few men and set out for Virginia to surrender with Lee's Army. However, the Army of Virginia surrendered before he reached his command, and Quantrill was mortally wounded in Kentucky. On June 6, 1865, at age 27, Quantrill died from his wounds at a Union hospital in Louisville. William Gregg survived the war and became a deputy sheriff for Jackson County, Missouri. He died on April 22, 1916, and is buried in Kansas City. Frank Smith surrendered to Union authorities and lived peacefully in Blue Springs, Missouri. He died on March 3, 1932. John McCorkle moved to Howard County and is buried there.

Jayhawker Jim Lane died shortly after the war. He committed suicide in 1866 after being caught embezzling federal money. However, many of the other prominent Kansans associated with the raid led honorable careers. Charles Robinson served as a Kansas state senator and later superintendent for the Native American Haskell Institute. Robinson was also appointed regent for the University of Kansas. He died on August 17, 1894. Charles Jennison became a Kansas state legislator and later, elected senator. He died on June 21, 1884. Col. Preston Plumb was elected U.S. senator, and Red Leg George Hoyt became the state attorney general. Capt. S. S. Clarke and Robert S. Stevens also became prominent politicians.

On November 15, 1866, the State of Kansas issued warrants for the arrest of 34 guerrillas believed to have participated in the Lawrence raid. Of this group, William Maddox was the only one to go to trial. Maddox was arrested and incarcerated in Ottawa, Kansas. Officials decided not to take Maddox to Lawrence as they feared he would be lynched. Maddox admitted he started out on the raid but became ill at Olathe and was forced to stop and recuperate. Maddox was unaware that Mrs. John Speer, whose two sons were killed in the attack, was in the courtroom packing a pistol with the intent of murdering him. While the jury was deliberating his fate, Mrs. Speer returned to her hotel room to nap. As she rested, the jury returned and found Maddox not guilty. Maddox's wife had already prepared a quick exit and waited outside the courthouse with two saddled horses. When the jury found Maddox innocent, he slipped out the back door, and the two rode off, never to be heard from again.

POSTMORTEM

It's clear that in the wake of the Lawrence attack that a biased Northern public used Quantrill's raid as a valuable piece of propaganda. To their credit, they have succeeded in convincing the historical record of the following: that the Lawrence raid was unprovoked; that their citizens innocent; the town defenseless; that no troops were in town; that women and children were murdered; and that those unarmed victims, men, women, and children, were randomly slaughtered by guerrillas.

William Gregg vehemently disagreed with this version and refused to apologize for his role in the raid. He believed the attack was retaliatory and that the victims were soldiers. He wrote, "We killed them in retaliation for the killings by the Redlegs, who came over into Missouri and raided our homes. It was war, that's all. Why talk about its being a raid on a defenseless town, there were five thousand troops on our heels before we crossed the Missouri line."[1]

In later years, Gregg expressed his anger about how the Lawrence raid was represented to the nation. He protested, "The Kansan has been the greatest traducer of Quantrill and his men. He has written chapter after chapter on the Lawrence Raid and the atrocities committed there, but never a word about what the Kansan did in Missouri. General Sherman said, and very truly, too, that war is hell and means to kill, and that is what the Kansan did when he came to Missouri, and what Quantrill and his men did when they went to Lawrence."[2]

Many years ago, my mother told me that there are 3 sides to every argument. The first is your side; the second is their side; and the third is the truth. The purpose of this study is for readers to be introduced to a side that has never been presented. Yet, it's up to the reader to determine what they choose to believe in. I would encourage students and researchers to resist believing everything they read in the historical record. The fact is, we are all biased. Consequently, it's important for us to conduct our own research and develop our own conclusions. If we do, we may yet find the true history of our fabulous country.

---

1   *Kansas City Times,* Aug. 20, 1910.

2   Gregg Manuscript.

Appendix

Victim And Survivor Analysis

POPULAR VERSION:

"The men killed were almost without exception, quiet, inoffensive citizens. They were loyal men, but not partisans. Very few had been in the army or had taken any part in the conflict."

— The Rev. Richard Cordley

CONFLICTING STATEMENT:

"There wasn't a citizen in the whole state of Kansas – they were all soldiers."

--William Gregg, Guerrilla

Appendix 1

14th Kansas Cavalry Victims:

- Allen, Charles R.
- Anderson, Charles
- Cooper, James F.
- Green, John R.
- Griswold, Walter B. S.
- Haldermann, Aaron
- Markle, David

- Markle, Lewis Cass

- Markle, Samuel

- Parker, Asbury

- Parker, Issac J.

- Riggs, Charles F.

- Speer, Robert

- Watson, John

- Waugh, William A.

APPENDIX 2

Victims with past military records (Free State Militia or Union soldiers) wrongly listed as civilians (Individuals in **BOLD** are suspected Red Legs because they deserted or resigned from the regular army in the Spring and early Summer of 1862, when the unit was being organized.):

- Allen, Elmore — Free State Militia

- **Allison, Duncan C. — Private, 7th Kansas Cavalry — deserted May 1862**

- Bell, George W. S. — 1st Lieutenant, 12th Kansas Regiment

- Brant, Randolph C. — Chaplain, 2nd Kansas Regiment

- Coleman, L. D. — Stubbs Rifles, Free State Militia

- Collamore, George W. — General — Local militia commander

- Crane, John L. — Capt. Samuel Hartwell's Company, Free State Militia

- **Dix, Ralph — 3rd Lieutenant — Capt. Samuel Hartwell's Company, Free State Militia — Red Leg suspect —**

captured at Johnson House

- Edwards, John — Private, 1st Kansas Colored

- **Finley, James B. — Capt. Samuel Hartwell's Company, Free State Militia — captured at Johnson House (reported as killed and reported as wounded, not killed)**

- Fitch, Edward — Stubbs Rifles, Free State Militia — Local Militia

- Gates, Levi — Scots Guards, Free State Militia

- **Gill, John B. — Bugler, 7th Kansas Cavalry — mustered out 1862.**

- **Green, John B. — 2nd Lieutenant, Company F, 7th Kansas Cavalry — deserted July 1862**

- Halderman, J. A. — Major, 1st Regiment Kansas Volunteers

- Hay, Chester D. — Stubbs Rifles, Free State Militia

- Holloway, three brothers — Privates, 14th Kansas Cavalry

- Johnson, Martin — Private, 1st Kansas Colored

- Jones, Samuel S. — Capt. John Wallis' Company, Free State Militia — known Jayhawker — killed in Fry's Livery Stable

- **Kimball, Frederick E. — Private, 7th Kansas Cavalry**

- Laurie, John — Recruit, 14th Kansas Cavalry, Free State Militia

- Laurie, William — Stubbs Rifles, Free State Militia

- **Leonard, Christopher — Private, 8th Kansas Infantry — discharged 1862 — Capt. David Horn's Company, Free State Militia**

- Little, John — Private, Company L, 9th Kansas Cavalry

- Loomis, Richard R. — Private, Company I, 2nd Regiment

Kansas Volunteers

- Lowe, Joseph G. — Captain, Free State Militia

- Markham, Sam — Private, 14th Kansas Cavalry

- Marvin, Sam — Private, 14th Kansas Cavalry

- Murphy, James — Private, Company F, 1st Kansas Regiment Volunteers

- **Murphy, Thomas — Private, 1st Kansas Infantry — mustered out June 1861**

- Murphy, Dennis — Undercook — 16th Regiment Kansas Volunteers

- **Nathan, Woodbury — Private, 2nd Regiment Kansas Volunteers — deserted 1862**

- **O'Neil, James S. — Sergeant, Company C, 2nd Regiment Kansas Volunteers — deserted 1862**

- Pope, George — Private, Company L, 1st Kansas Colored Volunteers

- Pratt, Caleb S. — 2nd Lieutenant, 1st Kansas Regiment Volunteers

- Purington, David N. — Private, Capt. Henry Learned's Company, Free State Militia

- Reynolds, Samuel — Private, Free State Militia

- Schmidt, Charles — German — Private, Free State Militia

- **Smith, Charles O. — Captain, Company A, 1st Regiment Kansas Volunteers — resigned July 1862**

- Snyder, S. S. — Chaplain, 2nd Kansas Colored

- Stewart, Henry — Private, Company L, 2nd Regiment Kansas Volunteers, deserted 1862

- Stone, Joseph — Union officer

- **Swan, Louis H. - co-owner Johnson House (Red Leg Headquarters)**

- Trask, Josiah — militia instructor, Free State Militia

- Watson, John — Private, Free State Militia

- Waugh, Addison — Recruit, 14th Kansas Cavalry

- Williamson, William T. — Private, Company D, 10th Kansas Cavalry

- Willson, Thomas J. — Private, 5th Kansas Cavalry

- Wilson, James — 14th Kansas Cavalry — listed as soldier and civilian

- Wise, Louis — Private, 8th Kansas Infantry

- Wood, James C. — Scots Guards, Free State Militia

- Woods, Andrew J. — 14th Kansas Cavalry — not listed as killed in all records.

- Zimmerman, John K. — 2nd Lieutenant, Lawrence Jaegers, Free State Militia

APPENDIX 3

Partial list of soldiers who were present during the Lawrence Raid and survived (Individuals in BOLD are Red Legs):

- Babcock, C. W. — General

- Bancroft, Edwin P. — Major, 8th Kansas Regiment

- Banks, Alexander — Captain, Provost Marshal

- **Buchanan, Wash — Red Leg**

- Clarke, S. F. — Captain, Assistant Adjutant General, Kansas Volunteers

- Clarke, Sydney S. — Major, Adjutant General's Department, Assistant Provost Marshal General

- Crackin, Joseph — Lieutenant Colonel, 1st Kansas Regiment, 3rd Regiment, Kansas State Militia

- Dietzler, George — General, 1st Kansas Volunteer Infantry

- Donnelley, John — Private, 11th Kansas Cavalry

- Earl, Ethan — Captain, 1st Kansas Colored

- **Eldridge, John — 7th Kansas Cavalry, Red Leg**

- Eldridge, Shalor W. — Colonel, Quartermaster Department

- Eldridge, Thomas — Major, 2nd Kansas Regiment Volunteers

- Ellis, George — 1st Lieutenant, 12th Kansas Cavalry

- Fisher, Hugh — Chaplain, 5th Kansas Cavalry

- Gilliand — Captain

- **Hampson, Captain Joseph T. - wounded at Johnson House.**

- Hazeltine, William — Private, 5th Regiment Kansas Volunteers

- Holt, Charles H. — 1st Lieutenant, 9th Kansas Cavalry

- **Hoyt, George — Captain, 7th Kansas Cavalry — Red Leg**

- **Hunter, George — Red Leg**

- Hutchinson, G. W. — Rev., Free State Militia

- Leis, George — 1st Lieutenant, 2nd Kansas Colored

- McAllaster, O. A. — Sergeant, Company A, 3rd Kansas Regiment

- **McFarland, Daniel — Private, 2nd Regiment Kansas Volunteers — mustered out 1861**

- **McFarland, John D. — Private, 13th Kansas Infantry — Deserted 1862**

- McFarland, Peter — Colonel, 7th Regiment, Kansas State Militia

- Miller, William — Private, 16th Kansas Volunteers, Company G, Kansas Militia

- Neill, Henry — Major

- Prentiss, Sylvester B. M. D. — Surgeon General, Kansas Volunteer Regiments

- Rankin, John K. — Colonel, 2nd Kansas Volunteers

- Rankin, William A. — Lieutenant Colonel, Assistant Quartermaster, Kansas Volunteers

- Reynolds, Charles — Chaplain, 2nd Kansas Cavalry

- Rothrock, Hiram — Private, 9th Kansas Cavalry

- Shannon, Andrew J. — Captain

- **Swain, Bloom — Captain, Red Leg**

- Swift, Frank — Colonel, 1st Regiment Kansas Volunteer Infantry — Kansas Militia Stubbs Rifles

- Twiss, Charles P. — Captain, Company I, 10th Kansas Cavalry

- Watson, James — Sergeant, 2nd Kansas Cavalry — Sergeant 7th Kansas Cavalry — deserted 1862

APPENDIX 4

Partial list of past soldiers or militiamen present in town who survived raid:

- Abbott, James B. — Free State Militia

- Adams, C. W. — Colonel, 12th Kansas Cavalry

- Allen, Lyman — Colonel, Free State Militia

- Bigelow, G. A. — Free State Militia

- Blood, James — Colonel, Free State Militia

- Brooks, Paul R. — Free State Militia

- Bullene, William — Local Militia

- Cracklin, Joseph — Lieutenant Colonel, 3rd Regiment Kansas State Militia

- Crocker, John G. — Stubbs Rifles, Free State Militia

- Christian, James W. — 1st Lieutenant, 9th Kansas Cavalry — resigned 1862

- Eldridge, Edwin — Free State Militia

- Emery, J. S. — Free State Militia

- Falley, E. R. — Sergeant, Free State Militia

- Fraizer, R. L. — Free State Militia

- Fuller, Dr. Alonzo — Captain, 2nd Regiment Kansas Volunteers — in charge of U. S. Hospital in Lawrence

- Griffith, G. W. E. — Free State Militia

- Gunther, Arthur — Captain, 2nd Regiment Kansas Volunteers — Free State Militia.

- Hay, George — Free State Militia

- Jenkins, J. W. — Jim Lane's Frontier Guards

- Kennedy, W. B. — 1st Lieutenant, Kansas State Militia

- Kimball, Samuel — Major, Free State Militia

- Leis, George – 1st. Lt. 2nd Kansas Colored

- Leonard, H. B. - Lawrence Militia

- Lindsey, Eliza — Captain

- Morrow, Robert — Free State Militia

- Petty, R. J. — Free State Militia

- Pratt, John — Adjutant, 2nd Regiment, Cavalry

- Prentice, Thad — Free State Militia

- Read, Fred — Local Militia, 3rd Regiment Home Guards

- Realf, Richard — Free State Militia

- Riggs, Sam — Local Militia

- Sands, J. G. — Kansas State Militia

- Savage, Forrest — Free State Militia

- Savage, Joseph — Free State Militia, Scotts Guards

- Searle, A. D. — Stubbs Rifles, Free State Militia

- **Sinclair, William T. — 2nd Lieutenant, Red Leg**

- Smith, C. W. — Free State Militia

- Smith, G. W. — Colonel, 5th Regiment, First Brigade of Lawrence Volunteers

- Speer, John — Free State Militia — Danite

- Spicer, Arthur — Free State Militia, Walker's Company

- Spicer, Newell — Colonel, 1st Kansas Cavalry

- Stevens, Robert S. — Kansas State Militia

- Storm, Ansom — Free State Militia

- Wilder, John — Major, 3rd Regiment Kansas State Militia

- Winchell, J. M. — Free State Militia (New York Times Newspaper Correspondent)

- B. W. Woodward, B. W. — Free State Militia

APPENDIX 5

Partial List Of Soldiers And Past Free State Militiamen With Residences In Lawrence:

- Allen, A. K. — Captain, 9th Kansas Cavalry

- Bassett, Owen A. — Lieutenant Colonel, 2nd Kansas Cavalry

- Beam, Leroy — Major, 14th Kansas Cavalry

- Bowles, John — Colonel, 9th Kansas Cavalry, 1st Kansas Colored

- Buchanan, Washington — 2nd Lieutenant, 9th Kansas Cavalry

- **Dean, John M.-- Sergeant — 1st Kansas Regiment — Red Leg**

- Dickey, Milton — General, Free State Militia

- Earl, George F. — Captain, 9th Kansas Cavalry

- Earl, William H. — 1st Lieutenant, 1st Regiment Kansas Volunteer Infantry

- Eldridge, Thomas — Major, 2nd Kansas Cavalry

- Gardner, Joseph — 1st Lieutenant, 1st Kansas Colored

- Gratton, John — 1st Kansas Colored

- Hinton, Richard J. — Captain, 2nd Kansas Colored

- Kimball, Warren — 2nd Lieutenant, 2nd Kansas Volunteer Infantry

- **Laing, John M. — 1st Lieutenant, 15th Kansas Cavalry — Red Leg**

- Lenhardt, Charles — 1st Lieutenant, 2nd Indian Regiment — Free State guerrilla

- Lovejoy, Charles J. — 12th Regiment, Kansas Volunteer Infantry

- Leonhardt, Oscar E. — Lieutenant Colonel, 1st Kansas Regiment — Free State Militia — Danite

- Mathews, William D. — Captain, Independent Colored Kansas Battery

- Miller, Josiah — Colonel, Judge Advocate, governor's military`staff

- Monroe, W. E. — Corporal, 9th Kansas Cavalry — Union Scout — captured Bill Anderson's sisters

- Moore, Amaziah — Captain, 9th Kansas Cavalry

- Moore, Horace L. — Chaplain, 2nd Lieutenant 9th Kansas Cavalry

- Nute, Ephraim — Chaplain, 2nd Kansas Colored

- Pearce, Lorenzo S. — Private, 2nd Regiment Kansas Volunteers

- Pike, Joshua A. — Captain, 9th Kansas Cavalry

- Pomeroy, Samuel — Major, 9th Kansas Cavalry

- Reeder, George — Private, 1st Kansas Regiment Kansas Volunteers

- Rosenthal, William — Quartermaster, 9th Kansas Cavalry

- Ross, Edmund G. — Major, 11th Kansas Cavalry

- Rothrock, Abraham — Private, 17th Kansas Cavalry

- Russell, Sheldon — Major, Adjutant, 8th Kansas Infantry

- Seaman, Henry — Captain, 5th Regiment Kansas Volunteers

- Searle, A. D. — Stubbs Rifles, Free State Militia

- Stewart, John E. — Captain, 9th Kansas Cavalry

- Sutherland, David — 1st Lieutenant, 1st Kansas Colored

- Tappan, S. F. — Colonel, First Colorado Regiment

- **Trego, Joseph — Captain, 5th Regiment Kansas Volunteers — resigned 1862 — Red Leg**

- Walker, Samuel — General, 5th Kansas Cavalry

- Whitman, Edmund — Captain, Quartermaster Department

- Wilder, John — Major, 3rd Regiment, Kansas State Militia

- Williams, James — Captain, Officer Black Regiment

- Wood, S.N. — General, Kansas State Militia

- Woodward, B. W. —Stubbs Rifles and Kansas Militia[1]

---

1 Sheridan – Adjutant General – Lowman – Cutler's History – R. G. Ellliott – Wilder – Griffith – Winchell – Riggs – Robinson, The Kansas Conflict – Armitage – Dary, David – Cordley, A Hist. – Crafton, Free State Fortress – Speer, Life of Lane – Nichols, Bleeding Kansas – KSHS, Index Kansas Volunteer Regiment Enlistments, 1861-1865 – Eldridge, Publications: KSHS - Clarke, S. S. - Holloway, John, History of Kansas – Lawhorn, Postmarked: Bleeding Kansas – Muster Out – "The Stubbs Rifles," Kansas Historical Quarterly, Vol. 6.- Robinson, Sara, Kansas: Its Interior and Exterior Life – Lowman, - Kansas Volunteers, For the Protection of the Ballot Box, 1857 – Sutherland's Lawrence City Directory for 1860-61 – Bailey, Lawrence D., A Graphic Look Description of the Quantrill Raid on Lawrence, Kansas – Boughton, J. S., The Lawrence Massacre: By a Band of Missouri Ruffians Under Quantrill by Reverend R. Cordley, Hon. Joseph Savage, J. G. Sands, F. W. Read Cordley, Richard, History of Lawrence, Sheridan – Adjutant General – Lowman – Cutler's History – R. G. E Roll, First Regiment, Infantry, Kansas Civil War Volunteers – The Daily Times, Leavenworth, Kan. - Stitt, William W., "Quantrill's Raid," Newspaper Article at Watkins Museum Kansas: From the Earliest Settlement to the Close of the Rebellion – Fisher, H. D., The Gun and the Gospel – Gihon, John H., Geary and Kansas: Governor Geary's Administration in Kansas with a Complete History of the Territory Until July 1857 – Robinson, Charles, The Kansas Conflict – Robinson, Sara T., Kansas, Its

APPENDIX 6

Black Civilian Victims:

- "Old Uncle" Frank

- "Uncle" Frank Dyre

- "Uncle" Charles Henry

- Black infant — Left in Eldridge House

APPENDIX 7

Killed By Mistake:

- Albach, George J. — Quantrill wanted him spared.

- Dulinsky, Sylvester — Quantrill wanted him spared.

- Martin, Robert "Bobby" — accidentally killed while dressed in father's Union uniform

- Stone, Nathan — Quantrill wanted him spared.

APPENDIX 8

German Victims

- Albrecht, George

- Alwes, George

- Brechtlesbauer, James

Interior and Exterior Life – Shea, John, Reminiscences of Quantrell's Raid upon the City of Lawrence, Kansas: Thrilling Narratives by Living Eye Witnesses – Connelley, William, A Standard History of Kansas and Kansans, Vol. 1 and 2 – Crafton, Allen, Free State Fortress: The First Ten Years of the History of Lawrence, Kansas – Cutler, William G., History of Kansas – Etcheson, Nicole, Bleeding Kansas: Contested Liberty in the Civil War Era – Holloway, John N., History of Kansas – Nichols, Alice, Bleeding Kansas – Roenigk, Adolph, Pioneer History of Kansas – Sheridan, Richard, Quantrill and the Lawrence Massacre, A Reader – Wilder, Daniel W., The Annals of Kansas.

- Brechtlesbauer, Joseph
- Engler, Carl
- Engler, John
- Ehlis, August
- Englesman, Philip
- Giffler, A.
- Kallmer, George
- Klaus, Frederick
- Klaus, William
- Klares, William
- Kleffer, W.M. R.
- Oehrle, George
- Pollock, Jacob
- Range, George
- Range, Samuel
- Reedmiller, Alois
- Reel, Samuel Jeremiah
- Wise, Louis

APPENDIX 9

Foreign Victims

- Allen, Charles R. — Canada
- Cooper, James — Ireland

- Eckman, Carl — Sweden

- Fillmore, Lemuel — Canada

- Giebal, Anthony — France

- Keefe, Patrick — Ireland

- Laurie, John — England

- Laurie, William — England

- Macklin (McClaine), Michael — Ireland

- Murphy, Dennis — Ireland

- Murphy, James — Ireland

- O'Neil, James — Ireland

- Schwab, John — France

- Williamson, William T. — Canada

APPENDIX 10

Abolitionist victims and their places of birth:

- Carpenter, Louis — New York

- Cornell, John A. — Massachusetts

- Dix, Ralph — Connecticut

- Dix, Stephen — Connecticut

- Eldridge, James — Massachusetts

- Griswold, Abner — New York

- Griswold, Jerome — New York

- Griswold, Watt — New York

- Hay, Chester D. — Connecticut
- Leener, Christian — New York
- Longley, Otis — Massachusetts
- Palmer, Charles — Rhode Island
- Palmer, Daniel W. — Rhode Island
- Perine, James — Connecticut
- Pope, George — Massachusetts
- Sanger, George N. — Massachusetts
- Sargeant, George — New Hampshire
- Stewart, Henry — New York
- Thorp, Simeon M. — New York
- Trask, Josiah — Massachusetts
- Tritch, E. P. — Massachusetts

Bibliography

PRIMARY SOURCES

Bailey, Lawrence D. "A Graphic Description of the Quantrill Raid on Lawrence," Garden City, KS: *The Kansas Cultivator*, 1887.

Barton, O. S., *Three Years With Quantrill: A True Story Told by His Scout John McCorkle,* Norman, Ok: University of Oklahoma Press, 1992.

Boughton, J. S. *The Lawrence Massacre: By a Band of Missouri Ruffians Under Quantrill, August 21, 1863*. Lawrence, KS: J. S. Boughton, 1885.

Britton, Wiley, *The Civil War on the Border*. New York, London: Knickerbocker Press, 1899.

Connelley, William E. "Interviews and Correspondence Related to Quantrill and the Border War." Topeka, KS: Kansas State Historical Society, Manuscripts Collection 16, Box 13.

Cordley, Richard.*The Congregational Record*. Lawrence, KS: Vol. 5, nos. 9710, Sept. & Oct., 1863.

_____, *A History of Lawrence, Kansas: From the Earliest Settlement to the Close of the Rebellion*. Lawrence, KS: E. F. Caldwell, 1895.

_____, "Quantrill's Raid or the Lawrence Massacre: August 21, 1863," Reproduced for the 125th Anniversary of Quantrill's Raid on Lawrence, Kansas.

_____, *Pioneer Days in Kansas,* (Boston, MA: The Pilgrim Press, 1903).

Dalton, Captain Kit, Guerrilla Captain of the Confederacy, Border Outlaw with Frank and Jesse James and Texas Ranger. *Under the Black Flag*. Memphis, TN: Reprint, 1995.

Davis, Adela Hunt, *True Stories About Pioneer Days, as Told to Her Grandchildren.* Lawrence, KS: Adela Hunt Davis, 1970.

Eakin, Joanne. "Recollections of Quantrill's Guerrillas: As Told by A. J. Walker of Weatherford, Texas to Victor E. Martin in 1910." First printed in the *Daily Herald,* Weatherford. Texas in 1910. Shawnee Mission, KS: Two Trail Genealogy Shop, 1996.

Fisher, H. D., *The Gun and the Gospel.*New York: Medical Century Company, 1899.

Fitch, Edward and Sarah. *Postmarked: Bleeding Kansas: Letters from the Birthplace of the Civil War, Pioneer Dispatches from Edward and Sarah Fitch.* Topeka, KS: Kansas State Historical Society, Purple Duck Press, 2013.

Gihon, John H., *Geary and Kansas: Governor Geary's Administration in Kansas with a Complete History of the Territory until July 1857.* Philadelphia, PA: King and Baird, Printers, 1866.

Gregg, William H. "A Little Dab of History Without Embellishment." Columbia, MO: The State Historical Society of Missouri, 1906.

_____, "The Lawrence Raid," typescript. 5 pages, Topeka, KS, Kansas State Historical Society.

Griffith, G. W. E. *My 96 Years in the West: Indiana, Kansas and California.* Los Angeles, CA: 1929.

Lewis, Lloyd. "Propaganda and the Kansas-Missouri War." *Missouri Historical Review*, No. 34, Pct. 1939.

_____, Lowman, Hovey E., *Narrative of the Lawrence Massacre on the Morning of the 21st of August, 1863: Prefaced with a Running History of the Early Settlement and after Experiences of the Historic City of Kansas.* Lawrence, KS: *Lawrence State Journal,* Steam Press Print, 1864.

Miller, George, D.D. *Missouri's Memorable Decade, 1860-1970: An Historical Sketch, Personal, Political, Religious.* Columbia, MO: Press of E. W. Stephens, 1898.

Miller, William. *Reminiscence, 1913.* Lawrence, KS: Spencer Library (Kansas Collection), Unpublished, 1913.

Phillips, William. *The Conquest of Kansas by Missouri and Her Allies: A History of the Troubles in Kansas, from the Passage of the Organic Act Until the Close of July, 1856.* Boston: Phillips, Sampson, and Company, 1856.

Ridenhour, Peter, "Quantrill's Raid, Aug. 21, 1863: *An Eyewitness Account,* from the Autobiography of Peter D. Ridenhour Who Survived the Raid," Lawrence, KS: The Douglas County Historical Society.

Robinson, Charles. *The Kansas Conflict.* Reprint, Honolulu, Hawaii: University Press of the Pacific, 2004.

Robinson, Sara T. *Kansas, Its Interior and Exterior Life: Including a Full View of its Settlement, Political History, Social Life, Climate, Soil, Productions, Scenery, Etc.* Boston: Crosby, Nichols and Company, 1856.

Shea, John. *Reminiscences of Quantrill's Raid upon the City of Lawrence, Kansas: Thrilling Narratives by Living Eye Witnesses.* Kansas City, MO: John Shea, 1879.

Smith, Frank. Manuscript: Notes taken by author from Frank Smith Manuscript by Dr. Albert Castel.

Speer, John. *Life of General James H. Lane.* Garden City, KS: John Speer Printer, 1896.

United Daughters of the Confederacy. *Reminiscences of the Women of Missouri During the Sixties.* Independence, MO: Two Trails Publishing, 2004.

Wheeler, Holland, "Statement of Captain Holland Wheeler," Spencer Library, Lawrence, KS.

SECONDARY SOURCES

Banasik, Michael E. *Cavaliers of the Brush: Quantrill and His Men: Unwritten Chapters of the Civil War West of the River, Vol. 5.* Iowa City, IA: Camp Pope Bookshop, 2003.

Beilein, Joseph Jr. *Bushwhackers: Guerrilla Warfare, Manhood, and the Household in Civil War Missouri.* Kent, OH: The Kent State University Press, 2016.

Beilein, Joseph Jr. *William Gregg's Civil War: The Battle To Shape The History of Guerrilla Warfare,* Athens, GA: The University of Georgia Press, 2019.

Blair, Ed. *History of Johnson County, Kansas.* Lawrence, KS: Standard Publishing Company, 1915.

Broughton, J. S. *The Lawrence Massacre by a Band of Missouri Ruffians Under Quantrill.* Lawrence, KS: J. S. Broughton Publisher, 1863.

Castel, Albert. *William Clarke Quantrill: His Life and Times.* New York: Frederick Fell, Inc. Publishers, 1962.

Collins, Robert. *Jim Lane: Scoundrel, Statesman, Kansan.* Gretna, LA: Pelican Publishing Company, 2007.

Connelley, William E. *Quantrill and the Border Wars.* New York: Pageant Book Company, 1909.

_____, *A Standard History of Kansas and Kansans.* Vol. 1 and 2. Chicago, IL: Lewis Publishing Company, 1918.

Crafton, Allen. *Free State Fortress: the First Ten Years of the History of Lawrence, Kansas.* Lawrence, KS: The World Company, 1954.

Cutler, William G. *History of the State of Kansas.* Chicago: A. T. Andreas, 1883.

Dary, David. *Lawrence, Douglas County Kansas: An Informal History.* Lawrence, KS: Allen Books, 1982.

Eakin, Joanne, and Hale, Donald. *Branded As Rebels.* Independence, MO: Wee Print, 1993.

Earle, Jonathan and Diane Mutti Burke, et al. *Bleeding Kansas, Bleeding Missouri: the Long Civil War on the Border.* Lawrence, KS: University Press of Kansas, 2013.

Etcheson, Nicole. *Bleeding Kansas: Contested Liberty in the Civil War Era.* Lawrence, KS: University Press of Kansas, 2004.

Fellman, Michael. *Inside War: The Guerrilla Conflict in Missouri During the American Civil War.* New York: Oxford University Press, 1990.

Findlen, Rose Ann. *Missouri Star: The Life and Times of Martha Ann "Mattie" (Livingston) Lykins Bingham.* Independence, MO: Jackson County Historical Society, 2011.

Freeman, Glen, Freeman Collection of Hesper, Kansas, history records, Spencer Research Library, 1912-1977. etext.ku.edu/view?docld=ksrlead/ksrl.kc.freemanglen.xml;route=ksrlead;query=

George, B. James Sr. *The Gregg Biography-Captain William Henry Gregg, Confederate and Quantrillian Officer, and good citizen: Dabs about the author of the "Gregg...little dab of history without embellishment."* Jackson County, MO: B. J. George Sr., 1973.

Gilmore, Don, "Total War, Fletcher Pomeroy, War Diary," typescript, unpublished manuscript in possession of author.

Goodrich, Thomas. *Black Flag: Guerrilla Warfare on the Western Border.* Bloomington, IN: Indiana University Press, 1995.

_____, *Bloody Dawn: The Story of the Lawrence Massacre,* Kent, OH: The Kent State University Press, 1991.

Herklotz, Hildegarde R., "Jayhawkers in Missouri, 1858-1863." *Missouri Historical Review,* Vol. 17, Issue 4, (July, 1923).

Houts, Joseph K. *Quantrill's Thieves.* Kansas City, MO: Truman Publishing Company, 2002.

Holloway, John N. *History of Kansas: From the First Exploration of the Mississippi Valley, to Its Admission into the Union: Embracing a Concise Sketch of Louisiana; American Slavery, and Its Onward March: the Conflict of Free and Slave Labor in the Settlement of Kansas.* Lafayette, IN: James, Emmons & Co., Journal Buildings, 1868.

Hulbert, *Matthew Christopher. Ghosts of Guerrilla Memory: How Civil War Bushwhackers Became Gunslingers in the American West.* Athens, GA: The University of Georgia Press, 2016.

Ismert, Martin E., *Quantrill-Charley Hart?,* Apache, OK: Young and Sons Enterprises, 1959.

Laird, Betty. "Quantrill Raid — A Compilation of Articles, Letters and other Material." Lawrence, KS: Watkins Museum Archives, August, 1988.

Leslie, *Edward E., The Devil Knows How to Ride: The True Story of William Clarke Quantrill and His Confederate Raiders.* New York: Random House, 1996.

Mink, Charles. "General Orders, No. 11, The Forced Evacuation of Civilians during the Civil War." *Military Affairs,* Vol. 34, No. 4 (Dec. 1970), pp. 132-137.

Minot, George. *The Statutes at Large and Treaties of the United States of America from December 1, 1851 to March 3, 1855, Vol. X.* Boston: Little, Brown and Company, 1855.

Monaco, Ralph A.II. *Scattered to the Four Winds: General Order No. 11 and Martial Law in Jackson County, Missouri, 1863.* Kansas City, MO: Monaco Publishing, LLC, 2014.

Monaghan, Jay. *Civil War on the Western Border: 1854-1865.* Lincoln, NE: University of Nebraska Press, 1955.

Monroe, R. D., PhD. "The Kansas Nebraska Act and the Rise of the Republican Party." Digital: Lincoln.lib.niu.edu/act.

Mullis, Tony R. "Soldiers Were Never On More Disagreeable Service: Peace Operations in Territorial Kansas and the Trans-Mississippi West, 1854-1956." Doctoral Thesis. Lawrence, KS: University of Kansas, History, 2002.

Nichols, Alice. *Bleeding Kansas.* New York: Oxford University Press, 1954.

Petersen, Paul. *Quantrill at Lawrence: The Untold Story.* Gretna, LA: Pelican Publishing, 2011.

Ponce, Pearl T. *Kansas's War: The Civil War in Documents.* Athens, OH: Ohio University Press, 2011.

Rafiner, Tom A. *Caught Between Three Fires: Cass Country, Missouri, Chaos and Order No. 11, 1860-1865.* Seattle, WA: Xlibris Corporation, 2010.

Roenigk, Adolph. *Pioneer History of Kansas: The Quantrill Raid, by W. K. Cone.* Chapter 11, p. 6. KanColl.org/books/roenigk/ch11.htm.

Sheridan, Richard B. (ed). *Quantrill and the Lawrence Massacre: A Reader* Lawrence, KS: Richard B. Sheridan, 1995. Parts 1-4.

Spring, Leverett Wilson. *Kansas: The Prelude to the war for the Union.* Boston: Houghton, Mifflin and Company, 1885.

Spurgeon, Ian Michael. *Soldiers in the Army of Freedom: The First Kansas Colored, The Civil War's First African American Combat Unit.* Norman, OK: University of Oklahoma Press, 2014.

Starr, Stephen Z. *Jennison's Jayhawkers: A Civil War Cavalry Regiment and Its Commander.* Baton Rouge, LA: Louisiana State University Press, 1973.

Webb, W. L. *Battles and Biographies of Missourians: or the Civil War Period of Our State.* Kansas City, MO: Oak Hills Publishing, 1900.

Welch, G. Murlin. *Border Warfare: In Southeastern Kansas: 1856-1859*. Pleasanton, KS: Linn County Publishers, 1977.

Wilder, Daniel W. *The Annals of Kansas*. Topeka, KS: Kansas Publishing House, 1875.

PERIODICALS

Bassett, W. J. Collection. Personal Recollections of the Kansas Episode from 1856 to 1860," Dated Sept. 28, 1896. Topeka, KS: Kansas State Historical Society.

Benson, Henry, "Manuscript of Quantrill's Raid Collections, 1913." Topeka, KS: Kansas Historical Society, MS Collection 159, Box 1.

Bidlack, Russell E., "Erastus D. Ladd's Description of the Lawrence Massacre," Ed. Burton J. Williams. *Kansas History: A Journal of the Central Plains,* Vol. 29, No. 2, (Summer, 1963).

Bissell, Sophia L. "See Those Men! They Have No Flag." *American Heritage Magazine*, Vol. 11, Issue 6 (Oct. 1960).

Bowen, Don R. "Guerrilla War in Western Missouri, 1862-1865: Historical Extensions of the Relative Deprivation Hypotheses," *Comparative Studies in Society and History.* Vol. 19, No. 1. (Jan., 1977).

Brown, A. Theodore. "Business 'Neutralism' on the Missouri-Kansas Border: Kansas City, 1854-1857," *The Journal of Southern History*. Vol. 29, No. 2, (May 1963).

Chase, C. M. Lela Barnes, ed. "An Editor Looks at Early-Day Kansas: The Letters of Charles Monroe Chase." *Kansas Historical Quarterly,* Vol. XXVI, Summer 1960.

Clarke, Henry S., "William Clarke Quantrill in 1858." Collections: *Kansas State Historical Society*, Vol. 7, 1901-1902.

Castel, Albert, "Civil War Kansas and the Negro." *The Journal of African American History,* Vol. 51, No. 2 (April 1, 1966).

_____, "Order Number 11: and the Civil War on the Border," *Missouri Historical Review,* July 1963, pp. 357-68. http://www. civilwarstlouis.com/History2/castelorder11.htm..

Dirck, Brian R. "By the Hand of God: James Montgomery and Redemptive Violence." *Kansas History, A Journal of the Central Plains,* Vol. 27 (Spring-Summer, 2005).

Doback, William A. Ed. "Civil War on the Kansas-Missouri Border: The Narrative of Former Slave Andrew Williams," *Kansas History,* Vol. 6, No. 4, Winter, 1983-84.

Eldridge, Shalor Winchell. "Recollections of Early Days in Kansas." Shalor Winchell Eldridge Collection, Kansas Collection, RH MS 128, Kenneth Spencer Research Library, University of Kansas, 1920.

Elliott, R. G. Shalor Winchell Eldridge ed. "The Quantrill Raid As Seen from the Eldridge House," *Publications of the Kansas State Historical Society Embracing Recollections of Early Days in Kansas.* Vol. II, Topeka, KS: Kansas State Printing Plant, 1920.

_____, News and Events Archives, Emporia State University, 2001.

Fox, S. M., "Early History of the Seventh Kansas Cavalry," Collections: *Kansas State Historical Society,* Vol. 11, (1909-1910).

Greene, Albert R., "What I Saw of the Quantrill Raid," *Kansas State Historical Society,* Vol. 13.

Harris, Charles. "Catalyst for Terror: The Collapse of the Women's Prison in Kansas City," *Missouri Historical Review,* Vol. LXXXIX, No. 3, (April, 1995).

Herklotz, Hildegarde R., "Jayhawkers in Missouri 1858-1863," *Missouri Historical Review,* Vol. 17, Issue 4, (July, 1923).

Jansen, Steve, "How Could It Have Happened?" *Douglas County Historical Society Newsletter*, July-August 2001.

Johnson, Samuel A., "The Emigrant Aid Company in Kansas," *Kansas Historical Quarterly,* Vol. 1, No. 5 (November 1932).

Johnson, Bingham, *The Midland Monthly,* (London, England: Forgotten Books reprint, 2009), Vol. 9: Illustrated; Jan-June, 1897.

Ladd, Erastus D. "Erastus D. Ladd's Description of the Lawrence Massacre." Ed. Burton J. Williams. *Kansas History: A Journal of the Central Plains,* Vol. 29, No. 2 (Summer, 1963), pp. 113-121.

Laforte, Robert S. "Cyrus Leland Jr. and the Lawrence Massacre: A Note and Document." *Kansas History: A Journal of the Central Plains,* Vol. 9, No. 4, (Winter, 1986/87).

Lewis, Lloyd. "Propaganda and the Kansas-Missouri War." *Missouri Historical Review,* No. 34, (October 1939).

Lovejoy, Julia Louisa. "Selected Letters from Kansas, 1855-1863." *Kansas Historical Quarterly,* Vol. 16.

Lutz, Rev. John J. "Quantrill and the Morgan Walker Tragedy," *Transactions of the Kansas State Historical Society,* Vol. 8, (1903-1904) pp. 331-351.

McAllaster, O. W. "My Experience in the Lawrence Raid," *Collections: Kansas State Historical Society,* Vol. 12, 1912, p. 401.

Martin, George. "First Two Years of Kansas," *Kansas Collections of the Kansas State Historical Society,* Vol. 6, pp. 123-124.

Mendenhall, Willard Hall, "Life is Uncertain: Willard Hall Mendenhall's Civil War Diary." *Missouri State Historical Review,* Vol. LXXVIII, No. 4, (July 1984).

Miller, William. "Reminiscences." Unpublished, 1-2 Kansas Collection: University of Kansas Libraries, (Lawrence, Kan.), 1913.

Palmer, H. E., "Black Flag Character of War on the Border." *Collections of the Kansas State Historical Society,* Vol. 9, 1913-1914.

_____, "The Lawrence Raid." *Collections of the Kansas State Historical Society,* Vol. 6, 1897-1900.

Pike, J. A. "Quantrill's Raid of Lawrence, Kansas: Statement of Capt. J. A. Pike Concerning the Quantrill Raid." *Western Historical Manuscript Collection,* Columbia,MO: University of Missouri.

Smith, Ed R. "Early Life of Quantrill in Kansas: How Quantrill Became and Outlaw." *Collections of the Kansas State Historical Society,* Vol. 7, 1901-1902.

Speer, John, "The Burning of Osceola, MO, by Lane, and the Quantrill Raid Contrasted." *Collections of the Kansas State Historical Society,* Vol. 6, p. 308.

Stephenson, Wendell Holmes. "The Political Life of General James H. Lane." *Collections of The Kansas State Historical Society*, Vol. III, 1930.

Stinson, Dwight E., "The Bloodiest Atrocity of the Civil War." *Civil War Times Illustrated,* December, 1963.

Unrau, William E., ed. "In Pursuit of Quantrill: An Enlisted Man's Response." *Kansas Historical Quarterly* Vol. 39, No. 3, (Autumn 1972), pp. 379-391.

Wellman, Paul, "Why Quantrill Raided Lawrence"

Weisberger, Bernard A. "The Newspaper Reporter and the Kansas Imbroglio." *The Mississippi Valley Historical Review,* Vol. 36, No. 4, (March, 1950).

Williams, Burton J. "Quantrill's Raid on Lawrence: A Question of Complicity." *Kansas Historical Quarterly,* Vol. 34, No. 2. (Summer, 1968).

LETTERS

John Dean to W. W. Scott, Jan. 26, 1879.

W. L. Potter to W. W. Scott, 1895.

R. S. Stevens to Dear Brother, Aug. 23, 1863.

Alexander Banks to Brother, Sept. 9, 1863.

Robert C. Stevens to Edward Leslie, Nov. 13, 1992.

Sarah Fitch to Ed Fitch Family, Sept. 2, 1863.

Cyrus Leland to Mother, Sept. 2, 1863.

Allen T. Ward to Dear Sister, Oct. 27, 1861.

Oscar G. Richards to W. E. Connelley, April 8, 1909.

John Stillman Brown to John L. Rupur, Sept. 1, 1863.

R. G. Elliot to Dear Sister, Aug. 24, 1863.

R. G. Elliott to Dear Sister, May 8, 1857.

Alex Case to Dear Sir, Feb. 4, 1915.

Samuel R. Ayres to Lyman Langdon, Aug. 24-27, 1863.

George E. Young to My Dear Father, Aug. 23, 1863.

Elizabeth S. C. Earl to Dear Brother, Sept. 22, 1863.

John G. Beeson to W. W. Scott, (no date).

Newspapers

The Squatter Sovereign, Leavenworth, Kan.

Kansas City Star, Dec. 28, 1938

Kansas City Star, Nov. 4, 1887

Liberty Tribune, Liberty, Mo., Nov. 22, 1861

Kansas City Star, Aug. 19, 1903

Kansas City Star, Aug. 21, 1939

Baltimore Sun, Sept. 1, 1863

Kansas City Star, July 19, 1903

BIBOLIOGRAPHY

Lawrence Kansas State Journal, July 2, 1863

Kansas State Journal, Nov. 6, 1862

University Daily Kansan, April 17, 1961

Leavenworth Journal, Aug. 6, 1863

Leavenworth Conservative, Aug. 4, 1863

The Independent Oskaloosa, Kansas, Aug. 29, 1863

Kansas City Post, Aug. 23, 1914

Washington Sentinel, March 9, 1878

Daily Journal-World, Lawrence, Kan., Aug. 17, 1940

Lawrence Daily Journal, Aug. 21, 1908

Liberty Tribune, Dec. 26, 1862

Council Grove Press, Sept. 14, 1863

Kansas City Times, Aug. 21, 1913

New York Times, Aug. 31, 1863

Kansas City Times, July 5, 1961

Newspaper Clippings: Stories of the Survivors: From Addresses made on Wednesday Evening at the Reunion in the Bowerstock Theatre

Daily Journal-World, Aug. 23, 1962

The Kansas City Star, Aug. 18, 1963

Kansas City Times, Dec. 8, 1975

Lawrence World-Journal, Lawrence: Today and Yesterday, Semi Centennial Memorial, Aug. 21, 1913

Quantrill's Raid: Watkins Museum Articles, Unknown Newspaper Clipping, Sept. 15, 1915

The Daily Times, Leavenworth, Kan., Sept. 4, 1863

New York Times, Sept. 22, 1863

The Daily Times, Leavenworth, Kan., Aug. 27, 1863

Kansas City Star, Sept. 25, 1898

The Higginsville Advance, Oct. 9, 1992

The Times Recorder, Oct. 24, 1982

Kansas City Times, Aug. 20, 1910

Oak Grove Banner, Sept. 22, 1905

The Daily Signal, July 19, 2017, Walter Williams, "The Key Facts About Slavery That the Left Conveniently Ignores"

Lecompton Union, November 1854

Herald of Freedom, Sept. 15, 1856

Morning Herald, Lexington, Ky., March 21, 1898

Kansas City Post, March 21, 1915

Kansas City Post, March 27, 1915

Betty Laird, "Quantrill Raid: A Compilation of Articles, Letters and Other Material from the Watkins Museum Archives," August 1988

Emporia State University, News and Events Archive, 2001

Daily Journal World, Commemorating the Semi-Centennial Memorial of the Lawrence Massacre, 1913

Lawrence Journal World, Aug. 23, 1962

Lawrence Journal World, Sept. 15, 1915

Council Grove Press, Sept. 14, 1863

GOVERNMENT RECORDS

Reports of the Special Committee on the Troubles in Kansas Territory, (1856), 34th Congress, 1st Session, No. 200

The War of the Rebellion: A Compilation of the Records of the Union and Confederate Armies. 128 Vols. And Atlas. Washington, D. C.: Government Printing Office, 1881-1901

Kansas-Nebraska Act, Primary Documents in American History, Oct. 26, 2017. https://www.loc.gov/rr/program/bib/ourdocs/kansas.html

State of Missouri, County of Jackson, Sept. 10, 1863, Philip Brown, Notary Public and Elijah McGee

www.Eudorahistory.com/civilwar

www.kansasmemory.org: List of Quantrill Raid Survivors, Lawrence, Kan.

ACKNOWLEDGMENTS

I'm thankful to God and Jesus Christ for giving me the perseverance to finish this project. I appreciate my wife's patience and support as I struggled through multiple disappointments. Special thanks to Dick Titterington, Beverly Shaw, Karen Stuth and Paul Petersen, for helping me with the manuscript. I'm also grateful to Steve Nowak and his staff at the Douglas County Historical Society, in Lawrence, Kansas, for their fantastic assistance.

ABOUT THE AUTHOR

James C. Edwards earned his M.A. in history from the University of Missouri-Columbia. He lives in Kansas City, Missouri.

Available From Shotwell Publishing

If you enjoyed this book, perhaps some of our other titles will pique your interest. The following titles are now available for your reading pleasure... Enjoy!

MARK C. ATKINS

WOMEN IN COMBAT
Feminism Goes to War

JOYCE BENNETT

MARYLAND, MY MARYLAND
The Cultural Cleansing of a Small Southern State

GARRY BOWERS

SLAVERY AND THE CIVIL WAR
What Your History Teacher Didn't Tell You

DIXIE DAYS
Reminiscences Of A Southern Boyhood

JERRY BREWER

DISMANTLING THE REPUBLIC

ANDREW P. CALHOUN, JR.

MY OWN DARLING WIFE
Letters from a Confederate Volunteer

JOHN CHODES

SEGREGATION
Federal Policy or Racism?

WASHINGTON'S KKK
The Union League during Southern Reconstruction

WALTER BRIAN CISCO

WAR CRIMES AGAINST SOUTHERN CIVILIANS

JAMES C. EDWARDS

WHAT REALLY HAPPENED? QUANTRILL'S RAID ON LAWRENCE, KANSAS:
Revisiting The Evidence

TED EHMANN

BOOM & BUST IN BONE VALLEY
Florida's Phosphate Mining History 1886-2021 and the Looming Ecological Crisis

DON GORDON

SNOWBALL'S CHANCE
My Kidneys Failed, My Wife Left Me & My Dog Died (I Still Miss That Dog!)

PAUL C. GRAHAM

CONFEDERAPHOBIA
An American Epidemic

WHEN THE YANKEES COME
Former Carolina Slaves Remember Sherman's March FROM the Sea

CHARLES HAYES

THE REAL FIRST THANKSGIVING

T.L. HULSEY

25 TEXAS HEROES

JOSEPH JAY

SACRED CONVICTION
The South's Stand for Biblical Authority

SUZANNE PARFITT JOHNSON

MAXCY GREGG'S SPORTING JOURNALS 1842 - 1858

JAMES RONALD KENNEDY

DIXIE RISING: *Rules for Rebels*

WHEN REBEL WAS COOL
Growing Up in Dixie, 1950-1965

NULLIFYING FEDERAL AND STATE GUN CONTROL:
A How-To Guide for Gun Owners

JAMES R. & WALTER D. KENNEDY

PUNISHED WITH POVERTY
The Suffering South – Prosperity to Poverty
and the Continuing Struggle

THE SOUTH WAS RIGHT!

YANKEE EMPIRE
Aggressive Abroad and Despotic at Home

PHILIP LEIGH

CAUSES OF THE CIVIL WAR

THE DEVIL'S TOWN
Hot Springs During the Gangster Era

U.S. GRANT'S FAILED PRESIDENCY

LEWIS LIBERMAN

SNOWFLAKE BUDDIES
ABC Leftism for Kids!

JACK MARQUARDT

AROUND THE WORLD IN EIGHTY YEARS
Confessions of a Connecticut Confederate

MICHAEL MARTIN

SOUTHERN GRIT
Sensing the Siege at Petersburg

SAMUEL W. MITCHAM

THE GREATEST LYNCHING IN
AMERICAN HISTORY: New York, 1863

CHARLES T. PACE

LINCOLN AS HE REALLY WAS

SOUTHERN INDEPENDENCE. WHY WAR?
The War to Prevent Southern Independence

JAMES RUTLEDGE ROESCH

FROM FOUNDING FATHERS
TO FIRE EATERS
The Constitutional Doctrine of
States' Rights in the Old South

ANNE WILSON SMITH

CHARLOTTESVILLE UNTOLD
Inside Unite the Right

ROBERT E. LEE:
A History Book for Kids

KIRKPATRICK SALE

EMANCIPATION HELL
The Tragedy Wrought by Lincoln's
Emancipation Proclamation

KAREN STOKES

A LEGION OF DEVILS
Sherman in South Carolina

CAROLINA LOVE LETTERS

JACK TROTTER

LAST TRAIN TO DIXIE

LESLIE R. TUCKER

OLD TIMES THERE SHOULD
NOT BE FORGOTTEN
Cultural Genocide in Dixie

JOHN VINSON

SOUTHERNER, TAKE YOUR STAND!
Reclaim Your Identity. Reclaim your Life.

HOWARD RAY WHITE

HOW SOUTHERN FAMILIES
MADE AMERICA:
Colonization, Revolution, and Expansion From
Virginia Colony to the Republic of Texas 1607 to 1836

UNDERSTANDING CREATION
AND EVOLUTION

DR. CLYDE N. WILSON

LIES MY TEACHER TOLD ME
The True History of the War for Southern
Independence & Other Essays

THE OLD SOUTH
50 Essential Books
(Southern Reader's Guide 1)

THE WAR BETWEEN THE STATES
60 Essential Books
(Southern Reader's Guide 2)

RECONSTRUCTION AND
THE NEW SOUTH, 1865-1913
50 Essential Books
(Southern Reader's Guide 3)

THE SOUTH 20TH CENTURY
AND BEYOND
50 Essential Books
(Southern Reader's Guide 4)

THE YANKEE PROBLEM
An American Dilemma (The Wilson Files I)

NULLIFICATION
Reclaiming the Consent of the Governed
(The Wilson Files II)

ANNALS OF THE STUPID PARTY
Republicans Before Trump
(The Wilson Files III)

JOE A. WOLVERTON, II

"WHAT DEGREE OF MADNESS?"
Madison's Method to Make
American STATES Again

WALTER KIRK WOOD

BEYOND SLAVERY
The Northern Romantic Nationalist
Origins of America's Civil War

GREEN ALTAR BOOKS (Literary Imprint)

CATHARINE SAVAGE BROSMAN

AN AESTHETIC EDUCATION
and Other Stories

CHAINED TREE, CHAINED OWLS: Poems

RANDALL IVEY

A NEW ENGLAND ROMANCE
and Other SOUTHERN Stories

JAMES EVERETT KIBLER

TILLER

THOMAS MOORE

A FATAL MERCY
The Man Who Lost The Civil War

KAREN STOKES

BELLES
A Carolina Love Story

CAROLINA TWILIGHT

HONOR IN THE DUST

THE IMMORTALS

THE SOLDIER'S GHOST
A Tale of Charleston

WILLIAM A. THOMAS, JR.
RUNAWAY HALEY
An Imagined Family Saga

GOLD-BUG (Mystery & Suspense Imprint)

MICHAEL ANDREW GRISSOM

BILLIE JO

MARTIN L. WILSON

TO JEKYLL AND HIDE

BRANDI PERRY

SPLINTERED
A New Orleans Tale

Free Book Offer

Sign-up for new release notifications and receive a **FREE** downloadable edition of *Lies My Teacher Told Me: The True History of the War for Southern Independence* by Dr. Clyde N. Wilson and *Confederaphobia: An American Epidemic* by Paul C. Graham by visiting FreeLiesBook.com. You can always unsubscribe and keep the book, so you've got nothing to lose!

Printed in Great Britain
by Amazon